EAST SUS

DOG FRIENDLY
PUB WALKS

DAVID & HILARY STAINES

COUNTRYSIDE BOOKS
NEWBURY BERKSHIRE

First published 2021
© 2021 David & Hilary Staines

COUNTRYSIDE BOOKS
3 Catherine Road
Newbury, Berkshire

To view our complete range of books please visit us at
www.countrysidebooks.co.uk

ISBN 978 1 84674 396 2

Photographs by David Staines

All materials used in the manufacture of this book carry FSC certification

Produced by The Letterworks Ltd., Reading
Designed and Typeset by KT Designs, St Helens
Printed by Holywell Press, Oxford

Contents

INTRODUCTION

There are few other counties in England that match the variety of scenery and history found in East Sussex. From the rolling hills of the High Weald to stunning coastal scenery where the South Downs meet the English Channel, East Sussex is a county of striking contrast, featuring countryside dotted with picturesque towns and villages, wide open marshes, beaches and majestic cliff top coastlines. This book capitalises on that variety together with the outstanding range of walks and scenery that is on offer – and of course what better companion to enjoy all this with than your dog?

We have chosen 20 canine friendly walks, centred on some excellent pubs that take in the best that the county has to offer. We have also incorporated places of history and interest so as to make them more memorable without detracting from the enjoyment of your dog.

A large part of the South Downs National Park lies within East Sussex, and we make no excuse that several of the walks are concentrated in this area. We will take you along cliff tops, beaches, seafronts, through historic villages, alongside wide open marshes and we even have a coastal town walk that includes the end of the pier, not to mention the possibility of a boat trip and a ride on the steepest funicular in the country.

Each of these walks has been specially surveyed for this book, focussing on dog friendliness. Even where we were familiar with the routes, we have walked them again to ensure all the information is as up to date as possible. Unfortunately we cannot rule out the fact that changes to paths, gates and stiles are not infrequent, if you find your route blocked by newly imposed obstructions, do not risk harming yourself or your animal. If in any doubt about either the progress or safety of the route, or where a path has become unclear, obstructed or for some reason non-existent always be prepared to turn round and just retrace your steps to the starting place.

Now be our guest as we take you and your dog through this wonderful county. Enjoy!

David & Hilary Staines

ADVICE FOR DOG WALKERS

The Countryside Code lists six steps to ensure your walk in the countryside is as safe as possible.

These are:

- Keep your dog on a lead, or in sight at all times, be aware of what it's doing and be confident it will return to you promptly on command.

- Ensure it does not stray off the path or area where you have a right of access.

- When using access rights over open countryside and common land you must keep your dog on a short lead between 1 March and 31 July, to help protect ground-nesting birds, and all year round near farm animals.

- Keep your dog on a lead around farm animals, particularly sheep, lambs and horses. This is for your own safety and for the welfare of the animals. A farmer may shoot a dog which is attacking or chasing farm animals without being liable to compensate the dog's owner.

- However, if cattle or horses chase you and your dog, it is safer to let your dog off the lead – don't risk getting hurt by trying to protect it. Your dog

will be much safer if you let it run away from a farm animal in these circumstances and so will you.

- Everyone knows how unpleasant dog mess is and it can cause infections, so always clean up after your dog and get rid of the mess responsibly – 'bag it and bin it'. Make sure your dog is wormed regularly to protect it, other animals and people.

Please show a sensible attitude when encountering other walkers, dog owners, sheep, cows and cyclists.

PUBLISHER'S NOTE

We hope that you and your dog obtain considerable enjoyment from this book; great care has been taken in its preparation. In order to assist in navigation to the start point of the walk, we have included the nearest postcode, however, a postcode cannot always deliver you to a precise starting point, especially in rural areas. Although at the time of publication all routes followed public rights of way or permitted paths, diversion orders can be made and permissions withdrawn.

We cannot, of course, be held responsible for such diversion orders or any inaccuracies in the text which result from these or any other changes to the routes, nor any damage which might result from walkers trespassing on private property. We are anxious, though, that all the details covering the walks are kept up to date, and would therefore welcome information from readers which would be relevant to future editions.

The simple sketch maps that accompany the walks in this book are based on notes made by the author whilst surveying the routes on the ground. They are designed to show you how to reach the start and to point out the main features of the overall circuit, and they contain a progression of numbers that relate to the paragraphs of the text.

However, for the benefit of a proper map, we do recommend that you purchase the relevant Ordnance Survey sheet covering your walk – details of the relevant sheet are with each walk.

It's also wise to check at the bar that there is no problem leaving your car in the pub car park before or after your visit.

1 ARLINGTON RESERVOIR

2 miles (1.6 km)

This is a short but pleasant walk in a setting which is frequently overlooked in comparison with some other more iconic landmarks close by. It's often an oasis of calm on busy summer days when visitors are flocking to other more well-known sites in the local area. The route starts from a local pub and features a circular walk around the reservoir which by its nature is almost flat. If you want a walk with a companion who may be less able to deal with any gradients you can park in the reservoir's own car park and just take in the circuit around the water.

Start & Finish: Berwick Station, Station Approach, Berwick, Polegate.
How to get there: The walk starts from Berwick Station which is on a minor road linking the A27 near Drusilla's Park with the A22 near Hailsham. The pub is immediately south of the level crossing opposite the station. **Sat Nav: BN26 6TB.**
Parking: At the pub or at the station. Very limited off-road parking provided you can find a spot that is both considerate and safe.
OS Map: Explorer OL25 Eastbourne & Beachy Head.
Grid ref: TQ526068.

THE PUB | **THE BERWICK INN** underwent substantial refurbishment in 2019. It now has a cosy modern pub and café atmosphere, set out as a coffee shop at the front and restaurant and bar at the back and side. It is clear that dogs are welcome when you see the sign by the door. If you want a walk with a really early start this might be the one for you as the pub provides coffee for morning commuters using the adjacent station from 7am!
☎ 01323 870018 ⊕ theberwickinn.co.uk

Terrain: The section of the walk from the pub to the reservoir is quite hilly, but the circuit around the water is flat and very easy.
Livestock: Horses in the fields between the pub and the reservoir.
Stiles and roads: No stiles.
Nearest vet: Chase Veterinary Centre, 89-91 Seaside, Eastbourne, BN22 7NL. ☎ 01323 639331.

The Walk

. . . .

① Turn right outside the pub and go over the level crossing. *The survival of so many historic features of the station has seen it featured as a little known national historic treasure in the media. The main station building is a rare survivor from 1846, whilst the most prominent feature is a signal box restored to Southern Railway green and cream colours together with authentic signage. It is thought to*

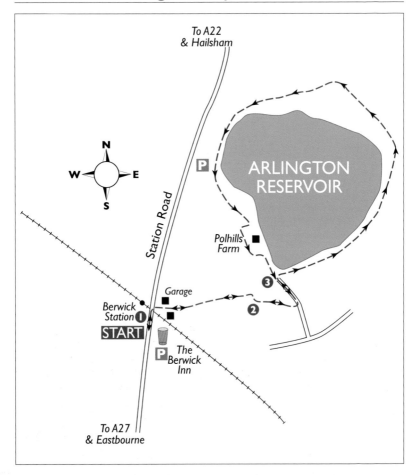

have been completed in 1879 whilst behind it stand some railway houses dating from the 1890s. Just before the petrol station take the footpath on the right-hand side. Go through the gate between the houses and then bear slightly left across the field. Go through the gate at the end and cross the next field. The footpath is a little indistinct but you are heading towards the other side of the field to the left-hand side of the electricity wires. Go through the gate at the other side and cross the little footbridge. Keep ahead and climb the hill keeping the fence line on your right-hand side.

2 At the very top look right and you will see a gate to your right, go through the gate and drop down the field. On the other side the exit from the field is in the right-hand corner. When you get to the corner go through the gate and turn

sharp left up the lane. After a short distance you will come to the reservoir. *The reservoir was built in 1971 and was created by damming the River Cuckmere, which previously meandered to the middle of the present-day reservoir. The Cuckmere is now channelled in a straight line just to the east. During construction a mammoth tusk, bison horn and a woolly rhinoceros skull (dating back ¼ million years) were found. Spoil from the excavation was spread around the site to create the landscape you see today.*

3 It's now a circular walk round the reservoir so it doesn't really matter which way you go. You might like to turn right here as this takes you out on the reservoir wall first and you get some good views across the water in one direction and towards the Downs and the Long Man of Wilmington in the other. When walking round you come to the reservoir car park where at certain times of the year there is a refreshment kiosk and water bowls for dogs. Whichever way you've gone round, when you come back to point 3 just retrace your steps back to the start.

2 ASHDOWN FOREST
3 miles (4.8 km)

There are **nearly 100 miles** of tracks and paths that criss-cross this classic area. Just like the more famous New Forest, it is not a forest at all as much of it is open heathland. The area is famous for its broad expanses of open land picked out with clumps of yellow gorse, and with its highest parts at over 700 feet above sea level, there are marvellous views in all directions. It's really popular with dog walkers, but there is some free roaming animal grazing and horse riding in the area. A board of conservation manages the forest and whilst you will find plenty of people out with dogs the board emphasises the need for vigilance and the usual reasonable guidelines for being out with your animal. Don't be put off – it's a great place for a dog walk.

Start & Finish: King's Standing Clump car park.
How to get there: Take the A22 either south from East Grinstead or north from Eastbourne. Just north of Nutley take the turn signposted for Crowborough. At the end of the road turn left along the B2026. The car park is on the right-hand side just before the B2188 turn. If coming from the eastern side of the county take the B2026 south through Hartfield and the car park is on the left just after the sharp turn signed for Groombridge. The local roads all have a blanket 40 mph speed restriction due to the danger of grazing animals unexpectedly obstructing the road. **Sat Nav: TN22 3JB**.

Parking: There is a free car park at King's Standing Clump, at the start of the walk. The forest car parks can get fairly full and there are alternatives further back along the road in the Crowborough direction. **OS Map:** Explorer 135 Ashdown Forest. **Grid ref:** TQ473301.

THE PUB

THE CROW & GATE was originally owned by the gatekeeper of Crowborough Gate, and travellers have been enjoying the hospitality here for over 200 years. Although dogs are not allowed in the restaurant area, it's very dog friendly with a large garden with water bowls and a big jar of dog treats on the bar.
☎ 01892 603461 ⊕ vintageinn.co.uk

Terrain: Undulating with some fairly steep drops and climbs. Broad tracks and paths.
Livestock: Potential to encounter livestock grazing and horse riders at any point.
Stiles and roads: No stiles. A short distance of road walking to access the pub.
Nearest vet: Starnes & Blowey, Fairfield House, New Town, Uckfield, TN22 5DG. ☎ 01892 764268.

The Walk

. . . .

1 Walk out of the car park taking the path on the far side opposite the car park entrance. Keep to the left of the clump of trees known as King's Standing Clump. *Although thought to be planted on an earthwork of megalithic origin, the clump of trees here marks one of the places where, in Tudor times, hunting parties would gather at an elevated spot and rather than tire themselves out by actually chasing their prey, they would have them pre-captured and driven past next to and below them, making the job somewhat easier. The Scots Pines came later, being planted in the 19th century.* Follow the path as it drops gently downhill and then slowly bears right as views of the valley open up on the left-hand side. *The Ashdown Forest had been a forest dating back to the Norman Conquest. By the year 1283 the forest had been enclosed by a 23-mile-long fence. Local people had the right to graze their livestock within the enclosure and this did much to suppress the growth of trees and scrub giving rise to the open views you see today.* Where three paths divert on the right-hand side in quick succession, keep going ahead.

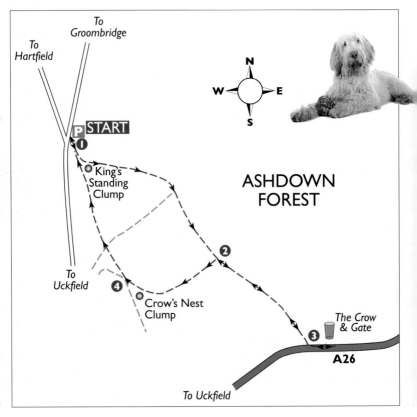

2 When you get to the bottom of the valley keep straight ahead and climb up the other side until you finally go through a livestock gate and out onto the main road. Turn left. Be very careful as for a short distance there is no pavement and only a very shallow grass verge to walk on. Very soon there is a grass verge on your right-hand side and then later a pavement on the left. On the left-hand side you will soon see the pub.

3 On leaving the pub retrace your steps to point 2. Now take the broad grassy path on the left-hand side as it climbs steadily up the hill. At the top keep right around another clump of trees. *This is Crow's Nest clump and has a similar history to King's Standing.* Follow the path straight ahead continuing in the same direction when another path merges in from the left.

4 Initially there will be some security fencing on the left-hand side. *The uninspiring looking land on the other side of the fence has a curious history. Situated on high ground it was chosen during the Second World War to house the world's most powerful radio transmitter. It was named 'Aspidistra' after a song popular at the time; the location was ideally suited to transmit messages to occupied Europe. Once the site had no further use as a wireless station, it later housed a Cold War bunker and then a police training ground.* You now follow this path straight ahead in the same direction and it will finally bring you back to the car park, this time with the King's Standing Clump of trees on your right-hand side.

3 BATTLE
3 miles (4.8 km)

Battle is a small market town that takes its name from the most famous land conflict to take place on British soil. October 1066 was the last time a foreign army ever mounted a successful invasion of England when Duke William of Normandy defeated Saxon King Harold to be crowned William the Conqueror ushering in the Norman rule of England. The walk starts from where William founded an abbey on the site of the battlefield to fulfil a vow he made before leaving France to mark the location if God granted him victory. The high altar of the abbey church is said to mark the spot where Harold died. Before or after the walk you can explore the substantial monastic remains and the peaceful meadow which was the site of the bloody battlefield. The site is now managed by English Heritage and contrary to some information both locally and on the internet dogs are definitely welcome.

Start & Finish: Battle Abbey, Butter Cross, High Street, Battle.
How to get there: From the A21 at John's Cross take the A2100 signposted for Mountfield Gypsum Works & Battle. Follow this road into the town, then turn left at the roundabout down into the High Street. Take the first left-hand turn onto Mount Street where you'll find the car park. **Sat Nav: TN33 0AR**.
Parking: There is limited on-street parking but there is a large pay and display car park off Mount Street. If you park here follow the alleyways from the right-hand corner of the car park into the High Street; there is no need to re-trace your driving route.
OS Map: Explorer 124 Hastings & Bexhill.
Grid ref: TQ747158.

THE PUB **THE ABBEY HOTEL** is right opposite the gatehouse and has undergone considerable refurbishment in recent years. Dog friendly in the bar and lower level. One of the bar staff accidentally trod on Jasper's tail and the next thing we knew he was very happily enjoying a compensatory bowl of gammon fresh from the kitchen!

☎ 01424 772755
🌐 abbeyhotelbattle.co.uk

The 15th-century **CHEQUERS INN**, just around the corner and down Upper Lake is thoroughly worth the very short walk. Dog friendly throughout, a great atmosphere and some of the best pub food we've had for a long time.

☎ 01424 772088
🌐 chequersinnbattle.com

For something very different, **THE POWDERMILLS HOTEL** close to point 3 on the walk is a beautiful Grade II listed 18th-century country house, once the residence of the owner of the adjacent gunpowder mills. It has an enviable reputation as being totally dog friendly (they can even stay) and, with pre-booking and agreement you can take an indulgent afternoon tea in one of the Georgian drawing rooms with your dog!

☎ 01424 775511 🌐 powdermillshotel.com

Terrain: Once you are out of the town square the route is all along footpaths, bridle paths and quiet lanes. Some steep gradients. Muddy after rain – bring the boots!

Livestock: Sheep encountered near Millers Farm and cattle around point 2.

Stiles and roads: There are three stiles between points 3 and 4. Only the largest of dogs might have difficulty getting through. If you need to avoid them, Powdermills Lane also links points 3 and 4. Some road walking at point 3.

Nearest vet: Senlac Vets, Mount Street, Battle, TN33 0EG.
☎ 01424 772148.

The Walk

. . . .

1 From the town square facing the abbey take the side road to the right of the gatehouse. Pass the English Heritage car park on the left and continue down the lane to the gate. Go through the gate and take the path down the field next to the left-hand tree line. Follow the path as it drops down and then rises again up to a three-way signpost in a field.

2 At the signpost bear slightly left following the Bexhill branch of the 1066 Country Walk. (Not the main 1066 Walk which carries on ahead.) Keep to the left-hand field boundary. Keeping in the same direction go through the gate near the bottom of the field and keep ahead. The path will broaden into a track as it climbs the hill out of the valley. At the top go through the gate, cross the lane and go through the second gate. Bear right along the path which runs adjacent to the lane at a higher level.

3 At the end cross the stile, cross over the road and walk down the lane opposite. A short distance later bear right down the private road which is also a public right-of-way as a footpath. Before you get to the oast house take the footpath on the right, cross the stile, keep to the left-hand side of the field boundary and go to the gate at the end. Cross over the stream to the next gate and bear left around the left-hand side of the field boundary. Halfway up the hill take the footpath on the left going over a stile. The footpath here appears to go straight across the next field but this is just a convenient short cut that walkers have taken. The right-of-way keeps to the right-hand field boundary. Just after the house on the right, go through the two gates on the right-hand side and out onto the lane. When you get to the lane, turn right and follow it to the far end.

4 At the end cross the road and take the path immediately opposite into the woods. Where the tracks diverge, bear left down the hill. Take the footpath past the right of the gate at the bottom. Cross the bridge and bear left around the lake. When the path leaves the lake follow the waymarked path up the slope leading out of the main woods. Don't follow the broader track to the right. Continuing ahead, go through the gate, cross the field and go through the gate at the other side, then turn right down the track. You are now on the waymarked main 1066 Country Walk. At the bottom of the valley you need to bear left up the clear space on the opposite hillside. The path is not waymarked at this point. *Although the site of the actual battlefield is beyond the trees up the hill to your right, this is one of the places where the Norman army would have grouped in advance. The Saxons chose the hilltop to their advantage*

and you can appreciate the gradient that the invaders would have had to fight their successful way up – as you will be climbing it too.

5 At the top, just beyond the brow of the hill you will be back at the three-way waymarker at point 2. Keep going ahead in the same direction retracing your steps to the start of the walk, bringing you back to the gatehouse in the town square. The Abbey Hotel is opposite and the Chequers is a right turn and then further along the High Street and into Upper Lake beneath the battlemented abbey walls.

4 BEACHY HEAD
6 miles (9.7 km)

This walk is a classic and takes in some of the most famous landscapes of the United Kingdom in an area very popular with walkers and visitors alike. You will be on the coast path along the cliff tops following the landscape as it rises and falls as you climb and then drop down the other side of two of the iconic Seven Sisters. The return gives you a quieter perspective as it diverts inland. There are plenty of things to see and do along the way. Don't attempt this walk on the weekend of the annual Eastbourne Air show unless you want to combine it with watching the displays (which makes a great day out) in which case you need to make a very early start indeed to cope with both travel and getting any kind of parking space. Be careful not to stray too close to the cliff edges on this walk. Use of a lead is advised on the cliff tops.

Start & Finish: Beachy Head Road car park.
How to get there: From the main Eastbourne – Seaford A259 road at East Dean follow the signposts to Birling Gap. The turn is at the bottom of the hill in the middle of the village whichever direction you come from. Continue past Birling Gap and follow the road as it twists and turns behind the cliffs. There are several smaller car parks along this road and it's useful coming in this direction as you can see what the parking is like in any of these, just in case the main car park at Beachy Head is full. **Sat Nav: BN20 7YA**.
Parking: Pay and display at Beachy Head close to the Countryside Centre, but if busy be prepared to double back to any of those car

parks that you have already passed. You can either walk back up the road to the start point or a useful tip if you find yourself too far back is to start the walk where it crosses the road between points 2 and 5 and just do the circuit from there.

OS Map: Explorer OL25 Eastbourne and Beachy Head.
Grid ref: TV590959.

Terrain: Some steep ascents and descents as you follow the cliff line up and down.
Livestock: Potential inland around point 5.
Stiles and roads: No stiles.
Nearest vet: Chase Veterinary Centre, 89-91 Seaside, Eastbourne, BN22 7NL. ☎ 01323 639331.

THE PUB

THE BEACHY HEAD INN is a large family pub serving food all day and much improved in recent years. One aspect of the pub which is curiously undersold is the superb unrivalled view of the South Downs and the coast across to Belle Tout Lighthouse, Seaford Head and Newhaven beyond. The pub started life as the Queen's Restaurant in 1880 and became the Beachy Head Hotel in the 1890s. During the Second World War it housed an advanced listening post when according to one local, nothing was served but mince and onions. There are dog water bowls inside and out and dog treats on the bar. It's a great pub in a great location, but

steer clear on air display days when it gets absolutely heaving. On one such day the queue time just to get a drink at the bar was over an hour – we know as we were in it!
☎ 01323 728060 ⊕ vintageinn.co.uk

The Walk

❶ Park at the Beachy Head Road car park next to the Countryside Centre. Cross the road and bear left at the seats on the other side of the road. Take the tarmac path that drops down to the viewing point, at the bottom there is a small war memorial and your first view of Beachy Head Lighthouse, although there will be better views further along the walk. *Beachy Head itself is the highest chalk cliff in Britain, rising 530 feet above the sea. Using 3,660 tons of Cornish granite the famous lighthouse itself was built in 1902 and replaced the old one at Belle Tout. Some years ago it was announced that there was no money available to keep painting its distinctive red and white stripes and the lighthouse would be left to weather to its natural granite grey. As a result a sponsored 'Save our Stripes' campaign raised the money needed to keep the structure's distinctive colours.* Continue up the tarmac path, ignore the first footpath on the left but then bear left out onto the broad grassy cliff top. You will pass a small observation point on the left and you will now have Belle Tout Lighthouse as your target straight ahead of you in the distance.

2 At the bottom of the next deep hollow there is a concrete trig marker set into the ground at the bottom of the valley. As you climb up the next steep ridge look back for a good view of Beachy Head Lighthouse. Keep going ahead over the top of the ridge and down again, then make the climb to Belle Tout Lighthouse. *The lighthouse was built in 1832. It wasn't a great success as fog would obscure the light on the clifftop whilst ships that had sailed too close couldn't see the light as it was blocked by the cliff edge. It was decommissioned in 1902 (and replaced by the famous Beachy Head light). It then became a tea house, was later bought as a family home in the 1920s but was very badly damaged in the Second World War. It was later restored again, then bought by the local council. In the 1980s the BBC bought the lease to use the lighthouse as a location for a TV series, thereafter it has featured in films and music videos. In 1999 due to the threat of continued erosion the whole 850 ton granite building was physically moved 56 feet away from the cliff face using hydraulic jacks pushing the building along load bearing beams.*

3 At times there is a small café in operation at the lighthouse. The path passes to the right of the lighthouse and you now drop down to Birling Gap. *It's another famous spot, but there have only ever been a few houses here, the*

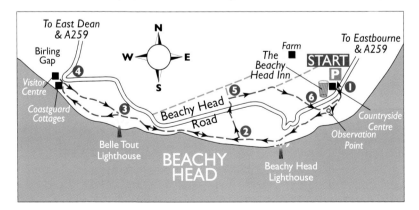

former hotel and a row of coastguard cottages built between 1800 and 1820. There were originally seven cottages, three have already succumbed to erosion, the last being demolished in 2014 after being left just six inches from the cliff edge. The cliffs here can sometimes erode at the rate of 1 metre a year leaving piles of fresh white chalk on the beach. The beach can be accessed by the large metal staircase, at low tide there are plenty of rock pools to explore. The National Trust has developed a visitor centre and tearoom in what was the former Birling Gap Hotel. The tearoom is open all day. Dogs are allowed in an area inside and outside at the tables at the front.

4 You now retrace your steps back up the hill past Belle Tout and return to point 2. There is no need to take the same path as you will see from the tops of the ridges there are all manner of different paths that you can take, some through the gorse bushes, which all take you back in the same direction. Back at point 2 you now turn left along the bottom of the gorse-filled valley. At the end turn right a few metres along the road and then take the first left-hand footpath. A short distance later turn right and you will see another footpath sign and a gate.

5 Go through the gate and keep to the path ahead of you with the fence line on your left-hand side. Note the low buildings of the Beachy Head Inn and the mobile phone mast behind it on the horizon, slightly to the right (remember where it is just in case for later).This is where you will be heading. About 100 metres later take a footpath that veers off to the right. It is a little indistinct. If you find yourself level with Bullock Down Farm on your far left on the other side of the valley you have missed the turn. Don't worry as on the horizon you will still see the top of the mobile phone mast. You are heading to the right-hand side of the low long clump of hedges to the right of the pub building. Once you've crossed the field, at the other side there are some benches at the side of the field just below the car park. It's a good place to stop for a rest and take in the view even on crowded days, as they are hidden from the car park and nobody seems to know they are there.

6 Cross the car park and the road and regain the grassy clifftop. Head to the left and you will soon be back opposite the starting point.

5 BODIAM
2½ or 5 miles (4 or 8 km)

This is a walk steeped in history and with a variety of things to see along the way. It features the famous 14th-century moated castle at Bodiam and gentle climbs up both sides of the wide Rother Valley. There is a chance for an extended walk alongside the gently meandering river. Two stiles make this walk only suitable for dogs that you can carry over. Try to start this walk as early as possible in the day. Firstly, parking will be easier but, more importantly, if you get there before the castle opens to visitors you'll have the still reflections and tranquil atmosphere to yourself.

Start & Finish: Bodiam Castle NT car park.
How to get there: From the A21 south of Hurst Green follow the signposted, left-hand turn for Silver Hill and Bodiam. Bodiam is three miles further on. When you drop down into the village the National Trust car park is on the left-hand side of the road and the Castle Inn is on the right. **Sat Nav: TN32 5UD**.
Parking: There are a handful of unrestricted parking spots next to the small village green. Otherwise there is a National Trust car park at the castle, although it is best to get there early as on busy days it can get full. Free for National Trust members. The Castle Inn has its own car park. Parking at Bodiam is restricted in the adjacent lanes for some way out of the village.
OS Map: Explorer 136 High Weald. **Grid ref:** TQ 783254.

EAST SUSSEX – Dog Friendly Pub Walks

THE PUB THE CASTLE INN enjoys a great position in the middle of the village and features a large garden at the side stretching as far as the river and the historic bridge. Dogs are welcome inside. It's a Shepherd Neame house and features a variety of their Kentish ales.

☎ 01580 830330 ⊕ castleinnbodiam.co.uk

On the other side of the road is the **NATIONAL TRUST CASTLE VIEW CAFE** which can get very crowded and dogs are only allowed outside. Midway on the walk is **THE HUB** café at Quarry Farm close to point 5. Open until 5pm daily it celebrates everything local from food and drink to crafts, and does not disappoint. With a contemporary look and feel, it is very dog friendly with dogs allowed inside on a lead and, without asking, we were offered a freshly filled water bowl.

☎ 01580 830932 ⊕ thehubquarryfarm.co.uk

Terrain: Moderate gradients up and down the valley sides, a variety of paths, some road walking with pavement or verge and some lesser used footpaths.

Livestock: The fields near point 6 are used to stable horses.

Stiles and roads: Several stiles, but two problematic if you cannot assist your dog over. Some road walking.

Nearest vet: Cinque Ports Vets, Cranbrook Road, Hawkhurst, Kent, TN18 5EE. ☎ 01580 752187 .

The Walk

. . . .

1 Go through the main castle entrance but keep to the left of the driveway. You will soon see some public footpath signs on the left-hand side. Follow the far left-hand path which gently climbs uphill with the castle on your right. Pass in front of the café building ahead of you and head for the far corner of the field. Please note that as long as you stick to the signed public footpath you do not have to pay the castle admission fee. If you wish to stray from the path and explore further then the fee is payable. *Bodiam's idyllic moated castle dates from around 1390 and was built with the King's permission as a defence against potential French invasion. However it's more likely that owner Sir Edward Dalyngrigge just wanted a 14th-century residential 'Grand Design' to impress – 700 years later he is still achieving that with over 150,000 visitors coming each year to have a look. Internally the castle was gutted after the civil war and abandoned until the 19th century.*

2 Cross the stile and head uphill. At the top of the hill bear left a few metres along the driveway following the yellow footpath waymarker. Then almost immediately cross the stile in the fence alongside another driveway opposite you. Drop down the hill and follow the path as it curves to the left. Go through the gate and then shortly take the gate on the right-hand side and drop down to the far end of the field.

3 At the lane turn right and then immediately left along the driveway, following the yellow footpath waymarker. Where the drive bears right, keep ahead through the gate and the next gate a few metres ahead. Then bear left through a third gate at the bottom of the hill and climb the hill. You are heading for a gap in between the houses. Cross the stile. This one is not dog

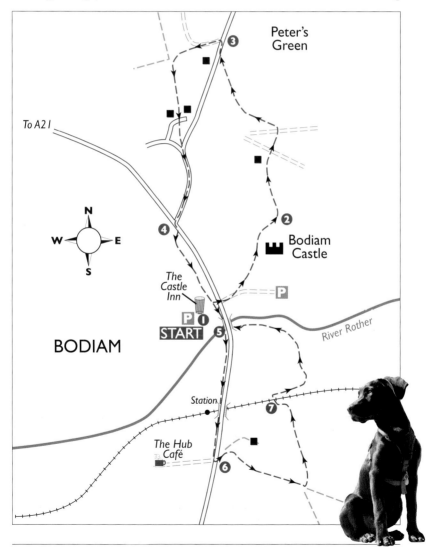

friendly – we had to carry our dog over it. Go up the path and then cross the cul-de-sac and follow the path through the wood opposite. Where the path diverges bear right in the woods. At the end, and when you emerge onto a residential road, turn left and then immediately turn right at the postbox. Now follow the pavement next to the road which drops down the hill back towards Bodiam village.

4 After you have turned left at the T junction take the path parallel to the lane on the right-hand side. Follow this to the very bottom and down to the Castle Inn. For the shorter walk return to your car but if you wish to continue then carry on past the pub to the bridge. *You would not believe it today but for 2,000 years the River Rother here was navigable by sea-going ships all the way from the English Channel. It is thought the Romans built the first bridge across the Rother hereabouts but the date of the ancient bridge in use today is uncertain. The Romans established a wharf on the river at Bodiam and commercial barges still used the river as far as the bridge right up until the 1950s. In summer you can take a gentle 45-minute cruise on a retired Royal Navy lifeboat down river to Newenden. Dogs go free.* ☎ 01797 253838.

5 Cross the river and keep to the pavement on the left-hand side. Go past the station and continue on up the grass verge on the right-hand side of the road up the hill. *This rural country station is the current terminus of the heritage Kent and East Sussex Railway from Tenterden. Opened as one of the country's first light railways in 1900 it was closed by British Railways in 1961 and reopened by volunteers in stages during the 1970s and 1980s. Hop growing was the major agricultural industry around Bodiam right up until the 1970s. The Guinness brewery farmed around 2,000 acres locally and it was claimed the amount of string used on the hop poles would stretch from Bodiam to New York. Behind the station there is* *a small exhibition showing what life was like for those who harvested the crop by hand, right up until the 1960s.*

6 Take the next left, opposite the wide entrance track to Quarry Farm. The concrete footpath sign showing the right of way is becoming very obscured by vegetation. (However if you want a refreshment break turn right instead along the track until you get to The Hub café below you on the right.) Returning to the main walk, having turned left off the road the access track here will soon bend to the left. On the bend take the footpath on the right. Again, this is getting quite obscured so keep a sharp look out – if you go beyond the bend and have an oast house facing you, you've gone too far. Follow the path over the stile, over the field, over the next stile and over the next field. The next stile may be problematic; the only way to cross on our visit was to carry our dog over it. Fortunately it is fairly low. Carry on down the next field keeping the hedgerow on your left-hand side. At the bottom, pass through the gate. Now turn left, it's not waymarked but the path keeps to the left-hand side of the field. Head for the left of the abandoned agricultural building at the far end. The path will be obvious where it crosses the river. Follow the path round when it gets to the railway line.

7 The path across the railway is marked by stiles either side and warning signs, but surprisingly there is no actual boarded crossing over the tracks, so be very careful not to trip on the rails. Having crossed the second stile turn right and follow the path around the outside of the large field in front of you. Keep to the footpath on the raised edge of the field; don't be tempted to cut across the marshy middle! The castle will be clearly in view so that you can orientate yourself around the field and back out onto the road close to the car park.

6 BULVERHYTHE
5 or 8 miles (8 or 12.8 km)

This is a walk of two great contrasts. The route takes you along miles of year-round dog friendly beaches with a foray inland along the paths of the Combe Valley Countryside Park; itself a great favourite for local dog walkers. There is also the lure of buried treasure – it's certainly here but impossible to get at!

Start & Finish: Oceanside Café @ Glyne Gap, Hastings Rd, Bexhill-on-Sea. **Sat Nav: TN40 2JU**.

How to get there: The start of the walk is roughly halfway between St Leonards and Bexhill but is easy to miss as you drive along the busy A259. It's situated on a bend in the road opposite the Esso petrol station on the Hastings side of the main roundabout on the east side of Bexhill.

Parking: There is a small free car park a few metres from the start of the walk at Glyne Gap. It is right opposite the Esso petrol station on the A259 just before the roundabout on the east side of Bexhill. If you get there early enough in the morning you stand a better chance of a space plus it's an excellent excuse to visit the café before you start. Access to the café is hard to spot from the road – it's through a low arch under the railway to the right of the public toilets, then just to the right once you are out on the beach. If you want to shorten the walk and cut out the first part there is limited free parking in Bridge Way at point 2 and more roadside parking on the north side of the A259 between points 2 and 3.

OS Map: Explorer 124, Hastings & Bexhill.

Grid ref: TQ764079.

THE PUB **THE MARINA FOUNTAIN** dates from 1837 and until 2017 was famous on the touring circuit as a bikers' pub complete with a Harley-Davidson mounted on the wall behind the bar. A couple of changes in management since has seen a change in direction with the pub now being recognised as one of the best community pubs in the area.
☎ 01424 446354   ⊕ marinafountain.co.uk

OCEANSIDE CAFE is a great place to stop either before or after the walk with a good value and inventive menu. If you try the breakfast burrito you probably won't need to bother with lunch! Open daily in the summer but check winter hours. ☎ 01424 218551 ⊕ oceansidecafe.co.uk

---

Terrain: Mostly flat. A combined cycle and footpath or along the beach by the coast, some narrow footpaths through the country park.
Livestock: None.
Stiles and roads: No stiles. About 100 metres or so of pavement walking alongside the busy A259.
Nearest vet: Cooper & Associates, 309 The Ridge, Hastings, TN34 2RA. ☎ 01424 751595.

The Walk

. . . .

❶ The walk starts from the Oceanside Café on the beach at Glyne Gap. When you are facing the sea turn left and take the coast path with the railway on your left and the beach huts on your right.

❷ When you get to the railway bridge on the left-hand side it's a good time to take a long hard look at the beach. *In 1749 the brand new ship the 'Amsterdam', owned by the Dutch East India Company, was on its maiden voyage from Holland to Java, loaded with 2.5 tons of silver when it came aground on the beach. It sank without trace into the sand and clay and was lost until the top of the hull reappeared in 1969. In the 1980s the Dutch authorities undertook official excavation but didn't get anywhere near recovering 2.5 tons of silver, most of which is thought to be still under the beach but unreachable. At exceptionally low tides (approx. 0.5 metres or below) the top of the hull is visible with $2/_3$ of the ship still intact below. It remains owned by the Dutch government and is a protected wreck.*
Cross the railway and walk to the end of Bridge Way. When you get to the main road turn right. Cross the road at the pedestrian crossing and keep walking along the pavement in the same direction. Take the first public footpath on the left-hand side. Don't take the first gap in the houses which leads to playing fields. Carry on a short distance until you've passed the first side road on your right-hand side and then take the next left down an access road leading to the playing fields, which

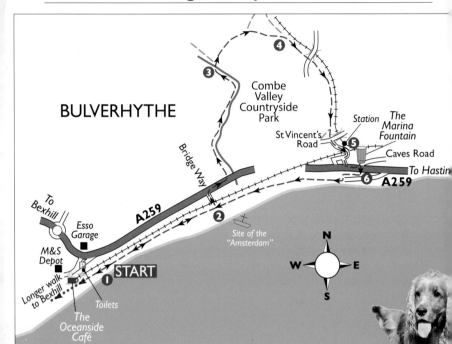

is also marked with a public footpath sign. Go to the end of the car park and walk through to the start of the playing fields keeping to the right-hand side. Follow the footpath signed Crowhurst and Worsham on the wooden countryside park marker No 1. Keep to the path with the watercourse on your right-hand side and a holiday village beyond. After a while, on the right-hand side at marker No 2, there is a large footbridge over the same watercourse. Don't cross this but keep going ahead. Further on you come out into a field to your left and a few metres further, on the right at marker No 53, cross the next footbridge over the stream.

3 At the other side of the bridge is marker No 3. Turn left at the end of the bridge and follow the path around, keeping the watercourse on the left-hand side. Don't cross the little footbridge on the left-hand side a few metres later, just keep going along the path right to the very end.

4 When you get to the end you will have the railway line high on an embankment in front of you. Turn right following the marker post to St Leonards and now keep the railway line high on your left-hand side. Where the paths diverge a few metres later, keep left. When you reach a road, cross it and carry on along the other side in the same direction. Keep ahead with the railway line on the left-hand side.

5 At the next road, cross over the pedestrian crossing and keep ahead along St Vincent's Road past the station on the left-hand side and bear right over the bridge. Turn right into West Hill Road and then left into Keats Close. At the end of Keats Close turn left onto the main road. You will pass the Bo Peep pub but on our last visit it did not allow dogs inside. Bear left into Caves Road and the Marina Fountain pub is immediately on your left-hand side.

6 From outside the pub cross the road and go straight into the gardens opposite. Turn right along the path through the gardens to the far end then bear left, cross the road and come out onto the seafront. Turn right at the seafront and you can either walk along the beach where dogs are permitted all year round or you can walk along the footpath and cycle track at the top of the beach past avenues of brightly painted beach huts. You now walk all the way back along the coast, past point 2 and back to Glyne Gap and the start.

If you would like to extend the day a little further you can walk the further mile and a half into Bexhill-on-Sea, returning the same way. Just keep going along the cycle path which will bring you to Bexhill's promenade, then keep to the seafront and you will come to the De La Warr Pavilion. *It was built in Art Deco style in 1935 following an architectural competition and was one of the first modernist public buildings in the country. Having fallen on hard times at the beginning of the century it was revitalised in 2006 with the help of lottery funding and is now a contemporary arts centre and Grade I listed.* Dogs are not permitted inside the main building, but they are very welcome (even if they've been in the sea) in the Colonnade café at promenade level. Open all day every day in the summer but may close some weekdays in the winter.
☎ 01424 819241 ⊕ bexhillcolonnade.co.uk

7 BUXTED PARK
2 miles (3.2 km)

This is a walk through the fields and grounds of Buxted Park, a stately home standing above the gentle valley of the River Uck a little to the south of Crowborough. Although the historic mansion is now a hotel, the footpaths through the grounds are free to access and it's a popular spot for dog walking. There are some great views, some lakeside walking and plenty to see along the way.

Start & Finish: St Margaret the Queen church, Buxted.
Sat Nav: TN22 4AY.
How to get there: Take the A26 south from Crowborough, after passing Heron's Ghyll turn left at the first roundabout signposted for Buxted, (if travelling from the other direction turn right at the 4th roundabout on the Uckfield bypass). Continue across the next crossroads (don't be tempted to turn right and take the first driveway which is blocked to vehicular traffic). Once over the crossroads take the next right, signposted to the church and hotel. Having passed the lodge you will see the bowls club and some parking spaces on the left-hand side of the road. Don't go any further otherwise you will find yourself in the hotel's private car park.
Parking: Next to the bowls club before you get to the church.
OS Map: Explorer 135 Ashdown Forest. **Grid ref:** TQ485231.

EAST SUSSEX – Dog Friendly Pub Walks

THE WHITE HART is an independent traditional pub and steakhouse where dogs are welcome. The recently refurbished bar combines clean open-plan design with some of the traditional features of an old English public house. Closed on Mondays.
☎ 01825 732068
⊕ thewhitehartbuxted.co.uk

> **Terrain:** Gently undulating paths, mostly through fields and a little woodland.
> **Livestock:** Potential for grazing sheep, horses and even geese on the bridle path between points 2 and 3.
> **Stiles and roads:** No stiles. There are a few metres of walking next to a busy road to access the pub. If you don't want to visit the pub you can cut this out or drive around the corner to the pub before or afterwards.
> **Nearest vet:** Starnes & Blowey, Fairfield House, New Town, Uckfield, TN22 5DG. ☎ 01892 764268.

The Walk

. . . .

❶ From the parking spaces by the church, go through the gate into the churchyard and bear left as you walk through the churchyard. *Note the old yew tree on the right-hand side, so old it is claimed to pre-date the birth of Christ.* Go through the gate at the end and follow the path as it drops down the hillside with the village of Buxted on the other side of the valley. Keep going to reach the bottom of the hill at the Second World War pillbox. If visiting the pub, the White Hart, bear left and follow the path through the gate and out onto the road. Take the pavement on the left-hand side as the road is usually busy. The pub is a short distance along the road on the left-hand side after you have crossed the River Uck.

❷ From the pub, retrace your steps back to the pillbox. Now keep ahead in the same direction following the broad path straight ahead. Keep the large tree line on your right-hand side. You will have views of the Buxted Park hotel on the hillside to your right. *The impressive Palladian mansion dates from the 1720s, and in the 1920s was owned by the designer of London's Savoy Hotel. At this time George V and Queen Mary were frequent visitors, and you can still stay in their grand bedroom!* However you may notice that it looks a little out of proportion. *In 1940 much of the house was damaged by fire, the top storey was never replaced due to the shortage of materials during the war.* You will soon have lakes on either side of the footpath. *These were dug as recently as the 1970s to stock fish on the orders of the Crown Prince of Abu Dhabi, a post-war owner of the mansion.* Cross or go around the little footbridge. You may encounter some geese at this point and the path here is also used as a bridleway for horses. A tall wall, the kitchen garden for the house, is on the right-hand side.

Go through the gate at the end and bear right but do not take the private service lane to the sharp right-hand side. Keep ahead with the fence line to your right and follow the main footpath as it goes into the trees. Go to the gate and follow the path as it drops down towards the stream.

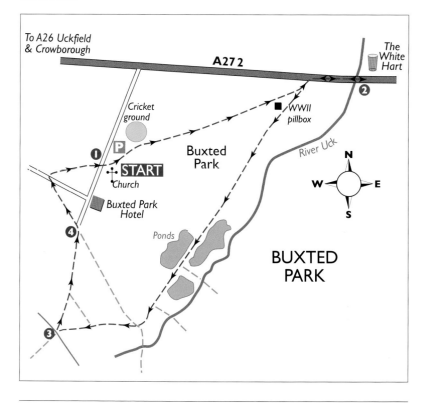

3 Do not cross the stream, at the gate turn sharp right and follow the path up the hill through the next gate and out into the field with the fence line now on your left-hand side. Continue up the path until you reach the end, where you have the hotel car park on the right-hand side.

4 Now bear left along the footpath heading downhill. At the end turn left down the drive and then, a few metres later, turn sharp right up the path towards the church. At the end turn left and you are back at the starting point.

8 CROWHURST
2½ miles (4 km)

Based around the tiny village of Crowhurst, this is a fairly short route but it takes in riverside and woodland paths and an RSPB nature reserve in a little known area with an interesting past. The village is first mentioned in 771 as Croghyrst and before 1066 the manor was owned by King Harold. Although sometimes portrayed as a Saxon stronghold it was certainly in the wrong place at the wrong time. It was the only settlement the Norman invaders encountered between landing at Pevensey and the site of the great Battle of Hastings only a few miles further inland. They completely destroyed it before the battle and afterwards the land was given to a French Lord.

Start & Finish: Crowhurst Recreation Ground, Sandrock Hill.
Sat Nav: TN33 9AS.
How to get there: From the A2100 halfway between Battle and the A21 north of Hastings take the signposted lane to Crowhurst. The lane twists and turns a fair amount. After you have passed the church on the right-hand side keep ahead (don't take the next right-hand uphill fork), shortly after you pass the pub on the right the car park is at the bottom of the hill on the right.
Parking: There is free parking in the recreation ground car park a few metres down the lane from the pub, or alternatively in the pub car park.
OS Map: Explorer 124 Hastings & Bexhill.
Grid ref: TQ759117.

THE PLOUGH sits in an enviable position on the hillside overlooking part of the village. There are log fires in winter and outside terraces in the summer. The bar areas are dog friendly - we received a welcome despite muddy boots and an even muddier dog!

☎ 01424 830310   ⊕ theploughcrowhurst.co.uk

Terrain: Mostly footpaths with a few short gradients. The low lying paths can get muddy in winter.
Livestock: Sheep and cattle in several of the fields.
Stiles and roads: A few stiles, but all with adequate dog gates or passages. Some road walking if taking optional route at point 2.
Nearest vet: Senlac Vets, Mount Street, Battle, TN33 0EG.
☎ 01424 772148.

The Walk

. . . .

❶ Turn right outside the recreation ground car park. Take the next left down Sampsons Lane. Take the first path on the left either through the gate or over the stile. Keep to the left-hand hedge line through the field. Cross the stream over one of the bridges and continue to the gate at the far end of the field passing a pond on the right-hand side.

2 At the gate turn right, carry on a few metres along the lane and then take the drive on the left between the manor house ruins and the church. *The gable end wall and empty trefoil-headed window on the left are all that remains of the 13th-century Manor House. Its builder, a crusader knight, was executed in 1259 having been convicted of the attempted murder of his employer, the Duke of Gloucester.* Go through the gate at the end and cross the field. Go through the next gate into the next field and keep going in the same direction, initially with the tree line on your right-hand side. Drop down to the bottom of the valley where a bridge crosses the stream. Don't cross the stream, bear right keeping the stream on your left-hand side and then go to the next gate a few metres ahead of you. You now keep going in the same direction keeping the main stream on your left-hand side crossing a few side bridges on the way.

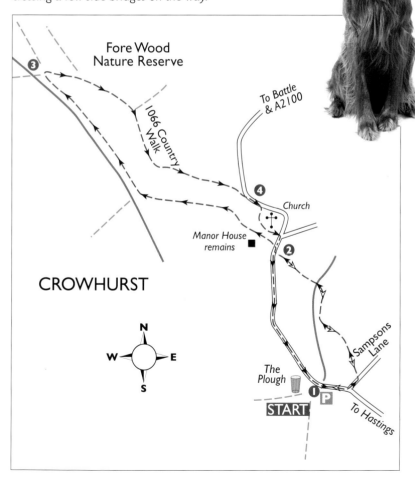

Fore Wood
Nature Reserve

To Battle
& A2100

1066 Country Walk

Church

Manor House
remains

CROWHURST

N
W — E
S

The
Plough

Sampsons
Lane

START P

To Hastings

3 At the far end, where the woods drop down to meet the stream, there is a stile with a dog gate. Cross the stile, turn right and immediately right again into the RSPB Fore Wood nature reserve. You are now back tracking the outward route but back through the woods along the 1066 walk. At the junction of paths a few metres later bear right and head up the hill. At the end of the wood go through the stile with the dog gate and keep ahead across the next field. You now just keep going in the same direction.

4 When you come out onto the lane turn right along the pavement. Take the next right through the gate into the churchyard. Follow the path round the churchyard. *Opposite the south porch is the ancient yew tree which some estimates put at being over 1,200 years old. It is claimed that in 1066 the invading Normans, whilst burning the village, hung the Reeve (a local official) from the branches of this very tree after he refused to reveal the location of valuables that the inhabitants had hidden from them.* At the other end of the churchyard turn right onto the lane and you will be back at point 2. You can either follow the lane all the way back to the start or retrace your steps back through the fields.

9 DITCHLING BEACON
4½ miles (7.2 km)

This walk takes you to the far western edge of the county, as well as to the highest point in East Sussex. Ditchling Beacon is a renowned beauty spot with fantastic views in all directions. Try to find a clear day to enjoy this great dog walking territory in order to take advantage of its spectacular views. This walk is best done in the morning as the car park is quite small and gets easily crowded on fine afternoons especially at the weekends.

Start & Finish: Ditchling Beacon car park. **Sat Nav: BN6 8XE**.
How to get there: From the A23 take the A273 in the direction of Hassocks. However, when you get to the village of Clayton take the B2112 signposted to Ditchling. Just before you get to Ditchling village take the dogleg right into Beacon Road. Once you start climbing the hill the road will twist and turn and get quite steep. Be careful as this punishing climb (used as part of the Tour de France when it started in England) is popular with very slow moving cyclists. When you get to the very top be ready to turn immediately right into the car park.
Parking: The car park at the Beacon is pay and display but free for National Trust members.
OS Map: Explorer 122 Brighton and Hove. **Grid ref:** TQ331130.

THE BULL'S location, on the crossroads in the middle of picturesque Ditchling, and the Great British Pub Awards certificates on the wall, are testimony to this pub's popularity. The main bar, in which dogs are welcome, manages to combine modernity with tradition whilst the well-maintained garden is a great place to sit out with views across the village towards the Beacon. Real ales from the excellent onsite Bedlam Brewery are on the bar. Dogs are requested to be on a lead in the garden and not to go into the kitchen garden area. ☎ 01273 843147 ⊕ thebullditchling.com

---

Terrain: Undulating with quite a steep climb towards the end. Long-distance footpaths, farm tracks or grassy footpaths, much of which cross open access downland.
Livestock: Chances of sheep along most of the route so you may want to have a lead ready. Potential for cattle between points 4 and 5.
Stiles and roads: No stiles. Plenty of gates but all are dog friendly. No road walking.
Nearest vet: Top Cat Veterinary Centre, 146 Mackie Avenue, Patcham, Brighton, BN1 8SB. ☎ 01273 504800 .

The Walk

. . . .

❶ Take the broad chalk path that leads away from the car park, then go through the gate marked nature reserve with the National Trust sign on the left-hand side. Keep going ahead up the gentle slope with good views on your right-hand side. You are on the South Downs Way. Keep to the broad path. Very shortly you'll reach the top of a hill with great views all the way round. *The hill is 814 feet above sea level at its highest point from which you can enjoy 360° views, and was once the site of an Iron Age fort. You can see the sea to the south, the Weald to the north and each side east and west the South Downs heading into the distance. The height of the hill made it an ideal site for a warning beacon which would be lit in times of imminent invasion – hence the origin of the name.* Don't take the path that leads downhill to the right-hand side but keep ahead on the chalk and gravel path with the fence line on the left-hand side. You now just keep going in the same direction. After a while you will pass a circular dew pond on your left-hand side. You will then be taking the next path on the left-hand side which you will come to at the top of the ridge ahead.

❷ Just after you have gone through another gate turn left at the signpost reading 'public bridleway to Chattri Memorial'. Go through the gate and take the path as it drops gently downhill. At the next gate, go through and cross the next field. *On your right you will still have some great views to the west and you will just be able to make out the tops of the Jack and Jill Windmills at Clayton.*

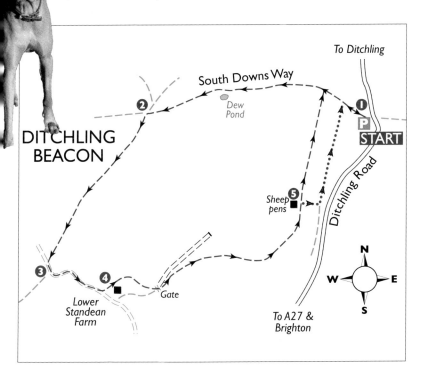

3 Just before the gate at the end of the following field turn left down the broad track which is signposted as a public bridleway. Follow it as it drops and twists down the hillside.

4 Just before the farm buildings take the path that veers left and go through the gate as the path curves up the hillside, through yet another gate at the top, and then down the other side into a broad valley. You will soon find yourself at the bottom of the often deserted valley known as North Bottom. Keep ahead along the track. After a short distance, go through the gate in the right-hand fence line and follow the path left as it gently climbs up the field, keeping the woods on your right. (If you have reached the gates where the track finishes you have gone too far, retrace your steps and you will find the correct gate shortly on your left.) At the far end of this field, go through yet another gate and through a small grove of trees on the other side. The path will now climb quite steeply up the hill ahead of you. When you get near to the top of the incline there will be another gate.

5 You can either keep ahead or, as an alternative, turn right a little further ahead. If you're taking the alternative route having turned right then take the next left and follow the path back to the South Downs Way. If you stick to the main route just keep going ahead past some sheep pens and at the end turn right when you come to the South Downs Way. Then there is just a short uphill climb back on the original route which will return you to the car park.

10 HARRISON'S ROCKS
2½ miles (4 km)

This route takes in a picturesque village on the county border with Kent. You can expect some good woodland paths and the walk features the massive sandstone outcrops of Harrison's Rocks, a rare and largely unknown geological feature of the landscape in this corner of the county.

Start & Finish: Groombridge Village Green. **Sat Nav: TN3 9QH**.
How to get there: The walk starts from Groombridge village which is on the B2110 south-west of Tunbridge Wells. From the west take the A22 out of East Grinstead and then the B2110 at Forest Row. Once in Groombridge go straight ahead at the mini roundabout and the Crown will be facing you as the road starts to climb past the village green.
Parking: Plenty of on-street parking in Groombridge village.
OS Map: Explorer 135 Ashdown Forest. **Grid ref:** TQ530377.

THE PUB

THE CROWN INN dates from 1585 and is a historical gem. During the 18th century smugglers used the inn as their headquarters until they were caught in 1749. Classic pub grub makes up most of the menu and local ales are served behind the bar. There are log fires to cosy up to and outside

seating overlooking the green for the warmer months. ☎ 01892 864742
🌐 thecrowngroombridge.com. Alternatively, try **JUNCTION INN** near the
station, which is known for its good food and service. Dogs are welcome
in the main bar and there is a large garden at the rear. ☎ 01892 864275
🌐 facebook.com/thejunctiongroombridge

Terrain: A variety of footpaths, woodland tracks and quiet roads.
Livestock: None encountered.
Stiles and roads: No stiles. Some quiet roads.
Nearest vet: Culverden Veterinary Group, Beechwood
Parade, Walshes Road, Crowborough, TN6 3RA. ☎ 01892 661650.

The Walk

1 The walk starts on the village green. *Whilst the tile-hung
houses overlooking the village green look peaceful and idyllic today,
between 1733 and 1749 Groombridge was home to one of the
most vicious, violent and notorious smuggling gangs in England. The
gang smuggled goods from the coast to London through a network of
rural byways with contraband hidden in remote country areas en route.
Groombridge, at the rough halfway point on the journey became a
centre of operations.* With your back to the Crown Inn drop downhill
to the far end of the green and carry on along the road and then
bear left just after the entrance to Groombridge Place. Through the village
you will soon see the Junction Inn.

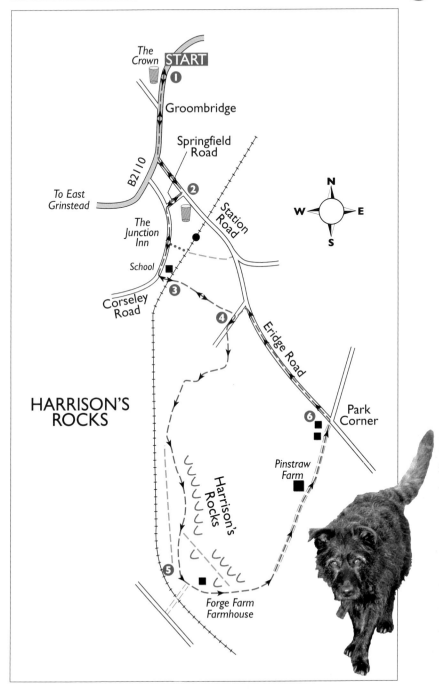

2 With the pub on the corner, turn right along Springfield Road. At the end turn left into Corseley Road. If you happen to be passing the turn for Gromenfield on the left and you hear a steam train it might be worth taking the path here and walking the short distance up to Back Lane Bridge where you get a grandstand view of what's happening at the station below you. *This is the heritage Spa Valley Railway which has an old-style country station in the village. If it's a weekend or during the school holidays you might be lucky enough to see a steam train at a few places on the walk. If you don't pass one you'll probably hear a whistle at some time.* Follow Corseley Road round until you pass the school on your left-hand side.

3 Take the footpath next to the school and cross the railway.

4 At the end of this footpath turn right along the lane. Follow the footpath around the car park (or just cut diagonally through it). At the south-west corner of the car park continue along the path following the waymarked sign. Follow the path out of the woods and continue along it once it has veered left. Where the paths diverge take the left-hand fork. On your right-hand side is the Spa Valley Railway again. You will now be passing along the base of the large sandstone outcrop known as Harrison's Rocks. *The rocks that you see today are millions of years old and were once the bed of a great glacier. For five million years* *sand and silt became tightly packed beneath ice becoming hard sandstone rock. Warmer weather saw the ice melt away whilst later land erosion revealed the hard rock we see today. The rocks take their name from an 18th-century owner, William Harrison who was one of the Wealden iron masters. Today it is hard to believe that iron was smelted in this part of the county for over 2,000 years. In the 1720s Harrison opened the rocks to inquisitive visitors. They are currently managed by the British Mountaineering Council and are very popular with rock climbers for training and practising their skills.* Carry on along the path until it comes to an end at a gate.

5 At the gate, turn left along the path where the railway line will now be to your right and below you. The path drops down to Forge Farm, at the bottom keep ahead where the right of way crosses through the frontage of Forge Farm Farmhouse. The exit is clear on the other side. The path now turns left and climbs back up the hillside, again passing some smaller sandstone outcrops. You will be walking on sandstone slabs as part of the path here. Keep ahead in the same direction and the path will become a track and then a farm access lane after passing Pinstraw Farm on the left-hand side.

6 Where it emerges at the picturesque little group of houses known as Park Corner, turn left down the lane. After a few hundred metres turn left down the access road signposted to Harrison's Rocks and a few metres later you will be back at point 4 from where you now retrace your steps back to Groombridge village.

11 HARTFIELD & POOH COUNTRY

2½ miles (4 km)

This is an easy walk, initially through fields and then down along the valley of the young River Medway, taking in the village of Hartfield and the hamlet of Withyham, each with a pub to choose from along the way. Hartfield's history goes back to Roman times and whilst the village has many houses that are 500 or 600 years old, it was in the 20th century that the village became more famous. Winnie-the-Pooh creator AA Milne moved here in 1925. All the places where Christopher Robin had his adventures with Pooh, Piglet and the other residents of 100 Acre Wood, were within the parish of Hartfield.

Start & Finish: The Anchor Inn, Church Street, Hartfield.
Sat Nav: TN7 4AG.
How to get there: The village is on the B2110 midway between Groombridge and Forest Row. Alternatively, take the B2026 turn halfway between Tunbridge Wells and East Grinstead on the A264.
Parking: On-street parking in Hartfield village or at the Anchor.
OS Map: Explorer 135 Ashdown Forest. **Grid ref:** TQ478357.

THE PUB

THE ANCHOR INN is now the only pub in Hartfield village but it's everything you would want from a dog friendly village local. It dates from 1465 and by the 16th century was referred to as a Manor House. In the 18th century it had fallen on hard times and was being used as the local workhouse, only becoming an inn in the 1890s. There are several drinking areas, an outside terrace from where you can watch the world go by and a more secluded garden. An adventurous guest ale policy provides ales from independent local breweries. ☎ 01892 770424 ⊕ anchorhartfield.com

THE DORSET ARMS in Withyham is an imposing building rich in history, dating from 1595, becoming a pub in 1735. It's named after the Dukes and Earls of Dorset and is today still in the hands of the descendants of that same family from the 16th century. Whilst much of the space inside is given over to dining it still retains a very traditional stone floored public bar with a water bowl for dogs. ☎ 01892 770278 ⊕ dorset-arms.co.uk.

There is also a dog friendly tea garden and shop at **POOH CORNER** on the main street. ☎ 01892 771155 ⊕ poohcorner.co.uk

---

Terrain: Rolling hills, nothing too steep. Mostly paths, and the flat Forest Way cycle and footpath.
Livestock: Sheep in the field after point 5. Potential for horses on the Forest Way.
Stiles and roads: Plenty of stiles, but all with dog gates or otherwise passable. A short distance along a quiet lane and one busy road to cross.
Nearest vet: Culverden Veterinary Group, Beechwood Parade, Walshes Road, Crowborough, TN6 3RA. ☎ 01892 661650.

The Walk

• •

❶ Turn left outside the pub, walk past the cottages and carry on along the track straight ahead. You are already on the High Weald Landscape Trail. After a few metres when you have the churchyard on your left-hand side take the footpath on the right. Cross the stile (there is plenty of space for dogs to go round the side) and then immediately bear left following the public footpath sign. At the end of the next field either go through the gate or across the stile and bare slightly left following the path next to the left-hand tree line. At the end of the next field, cross the stile. You now bear very slightly left across the next field. You now head downhill to the far corner of the second field.

❷ At the end of the field turn slightly right following the broad track and again follow it where it bears round slightly to the right a few metres later. You'll get a brief glance of Withyham church on your left-hand side through the trees. When you get to the next field a few metres later follow the public footpath waymarker as it bears left along the side of Forstal Farmhouse on the left-hand side. Follow the path and keep to the hedge line on the left-hand side. At the far end turn left through the gate onto the track, cross the stream, go over the stone bridge and then take the footpath on the immediate left.

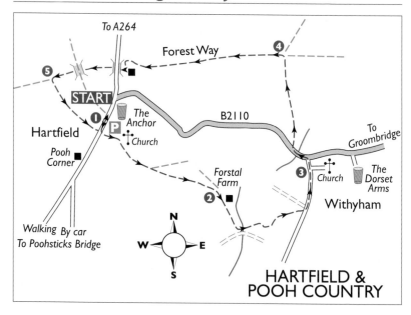

HARTFIELD &
POOH COUNTRY

If you happen to be following the route on an OS map don't be put off by the fact that neither the stream, the track or the bridge are shown on the map! Follow the path as it meanders through the woods and then out into an open field. Keep ahead in the same direction. Again, the Ordnance Survey map will show this path as a dead straight line when in actual fact it's not.

When you get to the far end cross the stile (again there is a dog gate) and then turn left down the quiet lane. This is now part of the Wealdway path.

❸ A little way down the lane take a right if you want to have a quick look at the church. There are some good views from the churchyard. Retracing your steps carry on down the lane to the far end. Take care at the main road. If you fancy a break, the Dorset Arms is a short distance up the main road on the right-hand side. To continue the walk turn left at the end of the lane, cross the bridge over the stream, and then turn immediately right. You now follow the path through the first broad field, past the gate post and across the second field.

❹ When you get to the trees and the Forest Way cycle route turn left. As you walk along the Forest Way you'll sometimes see Hartfield church in the distance ahead of you and to the left-hand side. Although you only get the occasional glimpse, you are sharing the valley bottom with the infant River Medway. The route is dead straight but where there is a kink, take the left turn then an immediate right and go underneath the stone bridge. Go underneath the next bridge as well.

❺ Then take the next footpath on the left, go across the stile and if you keep going straight ahead this will return you back to Hartfield and the start. The church tower can be your marker. Keep to the right-hand side of the cricket ground and the tennis court and you'll come out right opposite the pub. *If you want to find out more about the links between the area and the Winnie-the-Pooh stories just walk a short distance up the main street to the Pooh Corner shop on the right-hand side. The stories had an unlikely beginning; AA Milne owned a nearby farm and his son was Christopher Robin. The boy had a bear and other stuffed toys and Milne made up stories about their adventures. Quite by accident an international star was born! An out-and-back walk to the famous Poohsticks Bridge (or Posingford Bridge) is promoted from here. Alternatively take a short drive (take the first left, B2026) and turn right just after Chuck Hatch. Almost immediately on the right is a car park with an obvious broad path at the far end which will take you on the well-trodden route down to the bridge. Gather your sticks in advance, you won't find any on the ground around here!*

12 HASTINGS OLD TOWN

3½ miles (5.6 km)

This walk combines just about everything; cliff tops, a country park, a ride on the funicular, walks through parts of a town oozing with history and interest, the beach, pier, seafront and three cracking pubs along the way. Hastings has a unique atmosphere and the parts we go through have seen considerable change – for the better – in recent years. There's so much of interest that a few lines in a guide like this just can't do it justice. All we can do is mention a few dog friendly highlights.

Start & Finish: Rock-a-Nore Car Park, Rock-a-Nore Road.
Sat Nav: TN34 3DW.
How to get there: From the north take the A21 and from the west take the A259 to Hastings seafront. Keep going to the far end and where the main road bends left inland turn right along Rock-a-Nore Road under the cliffs to the far end where there is a large car park.
Parking: Public pay & display car park at Rock-a-Nore.
OS Map: Explorer 124, Hastings & Bexhill. **Grid ref:** TQ 827095.

THE PUB

THE STAG INN on All Saints Street is passed on the walk. The building dates from the 16th century and has two bars, an attractive back garden and roaring inglenook fires in winter. Said to be the former home of a witch and her two cats, the pub promotes itself as being 'especially dog-friendly "with a guaranteed" cuddle and fuss from the hosts', (we think that must be for the dog!).
☎ 01424 438791 ⊕ staghastings.co.uk

THE FIRST IN LAST OUT on the High Street, or 'The Filo' as it is locally known, is a Hastings institution and a few minutes' diversion off the walk. You'll find a traditional backstreet pub that also dates from the 16th century. A forerunner of the recent craft brewpub revolution, it started brewing its own beer in 1985 when only a handful of pubs around the UK were brave enough to do so. Jukebox and fruit machines are out, backgammon is in – it's that kind of place. Usually six Filo beers are on the bar. Good food served every day. ☎ 01424 425079 ⊕ thefilo.co.uk

THE DOLPHIN on Rock-a-Nore Road is conveniently located at the end of the walk. There has been a pub here since 1798, although the current building dates from the 1930s. Local fish, produce and ales are all on the menu. Fishing nets cover the ceiling and there is a small terrace outside where you can watch all the activity of the Stade. ☎ 01424 434326 ⊕ thedolphinpub.co.uk

Terrain: Paths and grassy walks in the country park with a fairly steep descent back into the town, pavements and beach. If the East Hill Lift isn't working it's a stiff climb up steps to the country park. Check the link via ⊕ visit1066country.com/things-to-do/cliff-railway.
Livestock: None.
Stiles and roads: No stiles. Some road walking but all with pavements.
Nearest vet: Cooper & Associates, 309 The Ridge, Hastings, TN34 2RA. ☎ 01424 751595.

The Walk

1 From the car park walk back down the road you have just driven along for a few metres to the bottom of the East Cliff Lift. *Take in the atmosphere of the fishing area known as the Stade, still home to the largest beach-launched fishing fleet in Europe. Unique to Hastings and built to the same design since the 1830s, the black painted three-storey-high net shops were used to stow nets and canvas sails. Dogs are welcome in both the Shipwreck Museum and the Fishermen's Museum.*

Almost opposite and set against the base of the cliff is the East Hill Lift, the country's steepest funicular railway which dates from 1902. The cars are original but have been converted from water balance propulsion to electricity. Take this historic funicular to the top. If the lift isn't working you'll need to walk to the top via a series of steps which are signed through the back streets further along the road. When you get to the top you'll have a great view of the old town below you and the coast stretching right round to Eastbourne and Beachy Head in the far distance. *Hastings has an ancient history. Around the time of the Norman Conquest it was a thriving fishing and trading centre. On top of the next hill you can see the remains of the first ever Norman castle built in England and on the seaward side the town's fishing fleet drawn up onto the beach. Until the 16th*

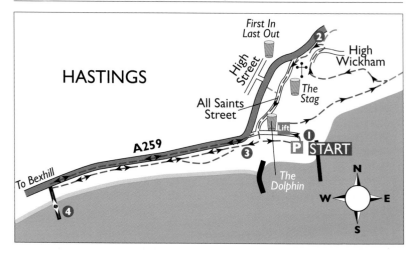

century Hastings was a powerful maritime centre, one of the famous 'Cinque Ports'. At the top of the lift turn immediately right up a short set of steps into the country park. Follow the right-hand field boundary. *The Hastings Country Park comprises nearly 700 acres of ancient woodland, grass and heathland together with dramatic coastline and cliffs stretching for five miles around Fairlight and Hastings. Most of the park has been designated a Special Area of Conservation and a Site of Special Scientific Interest.* Don't let your dog through the bushes as they mark the cliff edge. Continue ahead and eventually you will start to drop down towards the next valley, Ecclesbourne Glen. Do not keep descending but bear immediately left and sharp left again with a short sharp climb returning to the open fields that you've been walking around. Now continue with the boundary again on your right-hand side. When you pass an entrance to the park keep ahead in the same direction still keeping the hedge line on your right-hand side. At the next gap in the hedge line take the footpath that drops steeply down the side of the hill with a fence on the right-hand side. Keep following the path downhill. Then next to the large tile-hung house turn right. A few metres later this will become a road called High Wickham.

2 Continue down the road but where the road bends right, take the steps dropping down on the left. A few metres further on again turn left and drop down the steps. Carry on down the path to the very end and when you get to the road bear left round All Saints Crescent. Drop down the steps and turn left at the end. After you've passed the church on the left-hand side keep ahead down All Saints Street. Keep on the higher level walkway on the left-hand side which makes for an ideal traffic-free and dog friendly route. Here you can stop and take in the eclectic variety of ancient houses and cottages, some of which date from the 1450s. This part of the old town has formed the backdrop for numerous films and TV programmes and was the setting for TV's *Foyle's War*. Right on the route here

is the Stag Inn. Alternatively, if you'd like to visit a Hastings institution the First In Last Out is off the route but is only a few minutes away. Drop down Bourne Passage on the opposite side of the road, cross the main road, go down Roebuck Street and at the end turn right along the old High Street. Continuing the walk, carry on to the far end of All Saints Street, cross the road and walk ahead to the promenade.

3 When you get to the other side turn right along the seafront with the beach on your left and the amusement parks, boating lake and miniature railway on your right. Depending on the time of year you have a choice of walking along the beach itself or sticking to the promenade. The town of Hastings has undertaken a welcome clean up in recent years – as anyone standing here who has not visited recently will appreciate. Part of this has been the enforcement of dog control orders on the seafront. These are prominently displayed. At the time of writing the general rule is no dogs on the beach between this spot and the pier between May and September. Keep your dog on a lead on the seafront but dogs are fine off-lead on the beach beyond the pier. However, check the signs for the detail and any changes. It's a great walk along the seafront down to the Victorian pier and the good news here is that after a little recent local controversy dogs are now welcomed on the refurbished pier provided they are on a short lead. Once you are as far as the pier the next section of beach is dog friendly all year round anyway.

4 *The pier dates from 1872 and once featured a 2,000-seater art deco pavilion where The Rolling Stones, The Who, Pink Floyd and Genesis all played. It was all lost in a fire in 2010 which destroyed 95% of the pier's buildings. The simplified, redesigned pier was opened in 2016, receiving the prestigious Stirling Prize for architecture.* Once you have been down the pier retrace your steps back to point 3 but carry on past the end of All Saints Street. Hastings is well-known for its fish and chips and as you can see there is no shortage of cafés and restaurants. The Mermaid on the quieter section of Rock-a-Nore Road allows dogs at its outside tables with a water bowl on hand. A few doors down is the Dolphin and then you are only a few metres away from the car park.

13 HAVEN BROW & CUCKMERE EAST

3 miles (4.8 km)

This is a great walk in a world-famous location. Although it starts at the Seven Sisters Visitor Centre where the car parks are often crowded and there are invariably coach loads of thronging tourists, this walk soon takes you away from the well-trodden path up to where some of the best views in the county are on offer. This lesser-known route includes a 253-foot climb up to the top of the highest of the Seven Sisters. There is one stile at the top which larger dogs will have difficulty negotiating, but there is an alternative route. You can also link this walk up with the Seaford Head walk if you want a longer walk of nearly 7 miles.

Start & Finish: Seven Sisters Country Park Visitor Centre, Exceat.
Sat Nav: **BN25 4AD**.
How to get there: The visitor centre is on the main A259 Seaford to Eastbourne road, a few miles east of Seaford and close to Exceat Bridge.
Parking: There are two car parks at the visitor centre either side of the A259.
OS Map: Explorer OL25 Eastbourne and Beachy Head.
Grid ref: TV519995.

EAST SUSSEX – Dog Friendly Pub Walks

THE PUB **THE CUCKMERE INN** sits in a great location overlooking the South Downs National Park with views from its outside seats looking across the meandering River Cuckmere. Dogs are allowed in the bar area. Food is only served outside to the tables closest to the pub – which can get very busy on summer weekends. Take care if you choose to walk along the pavement next to the main road to get to the pub.

☎ 01323 892247 ⊕ vintageinn.co.uk/restaurants/south-east/thecuckmereinn
There is also a café in the visitor centre where dogs are welcome in the courtyard. However, there are not that many seats, and you have to wait to be seated. Alternatively, only a few minutes' drive away is **THE PLOUGH & HARROW** at Litlington. It has a secluded dog-friendly garden at the rear and dogs are welcome both inside and outside with water bowls and free treats on the bar. ☎ 01323 870632 ⊕ ploughandharrowlitlington.co.uk

---

Terrain: Paths and tracks with a fairly arduous climb and a steep descent.
Livestock: Plenty of sheep between points 1 and 3.
Stiles and roads: Only one stile but negotiable with a gap suitable for medium sized dogs. Larger dogs may need carrying over or take the alternative route. No road walking.
Nearest vet: Beechwood Veterinary Surgery, 37 Stafford Road, Seaford, BN25 1UE. ☎ 01323 893884.

The Walk

1 At the visitor centre there are two car parks on either side of the main road. Assuming you have parked in the main car park which is situated on the inland side of the main road you will need to cross the busy A259 and take the South Downs Way. The footpath is a few metres up the hill behind the bus stop. Turn left immediately after you've gone through the first gate, do not follow the broad concrete path. Follow the South Downs Way through another gate up the side of the hill. A short distance later follow the waymarker on the post and bear right. *Take in the view on the right. In 1846 the Cuckmere River was diverted into the straight channel which was built to drain the floodplain but the meanders which once formed the main river still spectacularly twist and turn down to the sea.* Go through the gate just beyond the top of the hill and then follow the path as it bears right looking down towards Cuckmere Haven. Soon a marker will confirm the way. You are heading to the far right-hand corner of the field at the bottom.

2 When you get to the bottom go through the gate, then cross straight over the concrete drive and go through the second gate facing you along the broad path. A few metres later take the left-hand turn marked South Downs

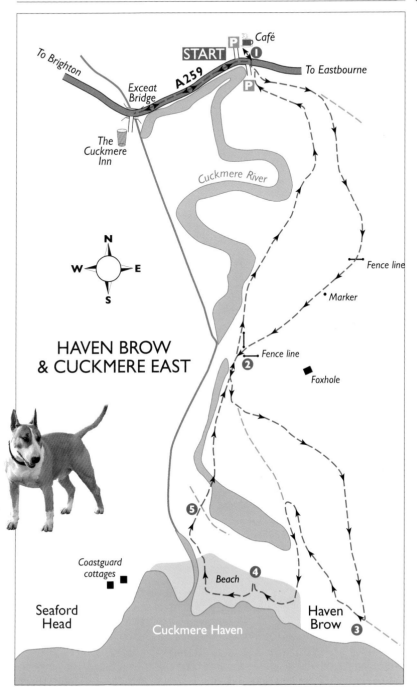

To Brighton

START

Café

P

P

A259

To Eastbourne

Exceat Bridge

The Cuckmere Inn

Cuckmere River

N
W E
S

HAVEN BROW
& CUCKMERE EAST

Fence line

Marker

Fence line

2

Foxhole

5

Coastguard cottages

Beach

4

Seaford Head

Cuckmere Haven

Haven Brow

3

Way and Park Trail. Don't go through the next gate but keep the fence line to your right and head up the hill. Don't go through the gate marked Park Trail (unless you want to avoid climbing Haven Brow, or have a large dog which will have difficulty in negotiating a stile at the top – if so, go through the gate and now head for the beach, catching up with the walk at point 4). Just keep on the South Downs Way. You are now climbing Haven Brow, the views just get better and better as you continue.

3 Take great care when you approach the top, the cliff edge will not be far away. Take your bearings from the three-armed public footpath sign. *You are now looking down on Cuckmere Haven high above the Coastguard Cottages which look tiny from this height on the other side of the bay. In the other direction the other six of the Seven Sisters march off in the direction of Belle Tout lighthouse whilst on your right, inland, the river meanders through its spectacular valley. In 2021 charitable plans to finance defences beneath the cottages were approved saving them from an existing policy that would have allowed them to fall into the sea. Rising sea levels and a suggestion to deliberately breach the canal may flood the adjacent grasslands and marshes and return the landscape to that of an estuary.* You now drop back down the hill in the direction of the beach. There is an obvious stile in the fence – with a medium-sized dog friendly hole. Although you're just heading for the beach, take great care when you are descending. After a very short while the land drops very sharply, almost at a 1:1 gradient. Although there are some informal pathways in the chalk – don't take them. They are just too steep and slippery. The safest way is to take the path on the far right-hand side which drops gently down the hillside and then at the bottom doubles back towards the sea.

4 Take some time to enjoy the beach, then you just need to walk towards the Coastguard Cottages on the other side of the bay. After a while you'll be stopped by the river, although at times in the summer it's sometimes little more than a wide stream. Make sure you don't cross it but keep it to your left-hand side and walk back up to the top of the beach.

5 At the top you will soon see the broad path that takes you all the way back to the start. When you reach the start of the broad path don't take the left-hand fork – although it looks like it's heading in the same direction it'll cut you off on the wrong side of the meanders. Just keep going ahead and you'll get some really close up views of the meandering River Cuckmere on the way back. One word of warning – in a few spots the path runs alongside brackish ponds which may contain algae which can be fatal to dogs if they drink the water. If you want to combine this walk with the Seaford Head walk, at the end turn left at the main road and keep along to the pavement until you reach the Cuckmere Inn. The route is shown as a broken orange line on the map.

14 HELLINGLY & THE CUCKOO TRAIL
2 or 6 miles (3.2 or 9.7 km)

You can use this walk as either a short circuit around the tiny village of Hellingly or you can extend it to include a longer out and back visit to the village of Horam. Hellingly is a picturesque cluster of old houses surrounding the church, parts of which date back to 1190. The walk features the Cuckoo Trail, part of the national cycleway network and built on the course of the former 'Cuckoo Line' railway from Tunbridge Wells to Eastbourne which took its name from the Cuckoo Fair which has been held at Heathfield, another nearby town, for over 600 years.

Start & Finish: Cuckoo Trail Parking, Station Road.
Sat Nav: BN27 4EU.
How to get there: The village of Hellingly is just north of Hailsham. About ½ mile north of the Horsebridge roundabout take the turn off the A267 onto the B2104 signed for Hellingly, then immediately turn left following the sign for Hellingly Church. Once in the village follow the sign for the Cuckoo Trail car park.
Parking: At the Cuckoo Trail car park off Station Road, signed as you pass through the village.
OS Map: Explorer OL25 Eastbourne and Beachy Head.
Grid ref: TQ 584121.

THE PUB THE WHITE HART is about ½ mile away in Lower Horsebridge. Sadly, there is no pub in the village itself. You'll find a traditional, family-run pub with a nice garden and good food. To get there drive back through the village but turn left onto the B2104 then right at the end and the pub is a few metres further down on the right. No food on Mondays.

☎ 01323 842221 ⊕ whiteharthailsham.co.uk

TPODZ TEA ROOM at Horam prides itself on its dog friendliness with dogs welcome inside and out. Open until 4pm, closed Mondays.
☎ 01435 810310 ⊕ horamemporium.co.uk

Terrain: Flat but with steps for access in places.
Livestock: Potential for sheep and cattle between points 2 and 3.
Stiles and roads: Only one stile but with a dog friendly gate. Some road walking.
Nearest vet: Downwood Veterinary Centre, 6 High Street, Horam, TN21 0EJ. ☎ 01435 812152.

The Walk

❶ Leave the car park at the far end. You immediately come to a fragment of the original platform of Hellingly Station. This is your first indication of the heritage of the trail. *The railway closed to passengers in 1965 (by then it was only being used by 250 people each day) and for goods trains in 1968. In 1994 the route was tarmacked and converted into the trail which runs for 11 miles from Heathfield into the outskirts of Eastbourne. Benches and sculptures have been placed along the route which is used by 250,000 walkers, cyclists and horse riders every year.* The old station building on the right has been finely restored as a private residence and is now mostly screened from view by trees and bushes. Turn left under the bridge. Keep ahead along the trail. After you have passed under the next stone bridge walk on to the second footpath on the left-hand side where you have a choice.

❷ For the long walk, keep ahead along the Cuckoo Trail** (see p69 for the longer route). For the shorter walk turn left here, walk up the steps and cross the stile. There is a convenient dog gate. Take the path diagonally left across the field. Cross the field, go through the gate, cross the next field and

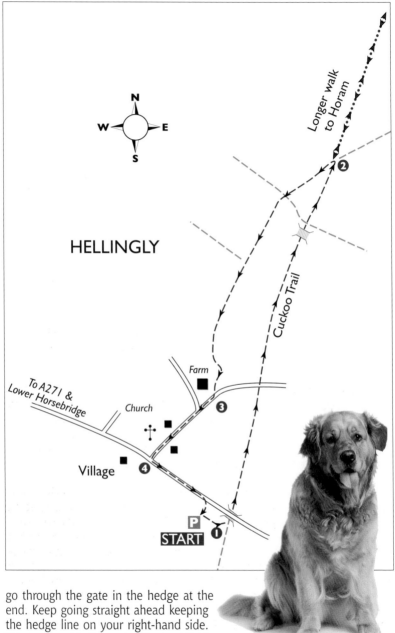

N
W E
S

Longer walk to Horam

HELLINGLY

Cuckoo Trail

Farm

To A271 & Lower Horsebridge

Church

Village

START

go through the gate in the hedge at the end. Keep going straight ahead keeping the hedge line on your right-hand side. When you get to the end of the next field go through the three gates in front of you, crossing the stream bed, and keep going ahead in the same direction. At the end of

the following field, go through the two gates then keep to the left-hand hedge line. You're heading to the left of the farm buildings. Skirt the farm through the series of gates on the left-hand side.

3 When you come to Mill Lane turn right and a few metres later bear slightly left and keep walking along the lane into the village. Skirt the church on the right-hand side. Alternatively you can walk through the churchyard.

4 At the end of the lane turn left into Station Road. Continue along the lane until you are back at the car park on the right-hand side.

** **If you are taking the long walk**, the next section will be a straightforward out and back 4-mile return walk to the village of Horam. When you get to the outskirts of Horam village follow the Cuckoo Trail signs through the residential development until you get to the remains of the station platform. *A couple of the distinctive old platform lamp posts and the concrete mounting for the station name board are remarkable survivors as they last saw a train over half a century ago. The actual signs are modern replicas. Your reward for the extra walk will be a visit to the Tpodz Tea Room. Just go up the steps opposite the name board and at the top it's on the opposite side of the road. It is in the premises of the former iconic (to bikers at least) Wessons Café but remains resolutely dog friendly inside and out. Great cakes and Jasper was spoilt with complimentary sausage on the house.* To return, head back across the road, back down the steps and retrace your route back to point 2.

On the signpost:
LAUGHTON CHURCH
RIPE   2

SHORTGATE 1¼
HA...ND 2¼
B2124

B2124
RINGMER
LEWES

HAILSHAM   7
EASTBOURNE 14
BATTLE   18

15 LAUGHTON
1½ miles (2.4 km)

Laughton is where the South Downs meet the woodland of the Sussex Weald. This is not a very long walk but it's a classic, with a route that takes you through the woods and has a really good pub to start and finish. Perhaps this is ideal on a winter's day for a quick outing either before or after Sunday lunch?

The little village has led a fairly uneventful existence over the centuries, its main claim to fame being the capture of the King of France by a local knight at the Battle of Poitiers. The village church dates from 1229 but as you stand in the middle of the village at the start of the walk, there is no sign of it – apart from a sign to it.

Start & Finish: The Roebuck Inn, Laughton. **Sat Nav: BN8 6BG**.
How to get there: Laughton is on the B2124 a few miles east of Ringmer. The pub is at the crossroads in the middle of the village.
Parking: Either at the pub or there is on-street parking on Shortgate Lane or in the village near the Post Office.
OS Map: Explorer OL25 Eastbourne & Beachy Head.
Grid ref: TQ502132.

THE PUB | **THE ROEBUCK INN** reopened in 2021 under new local management and is now a family run pub, aiming to be 'proper local' as opposed to a gastropub – always a welcome sign if you turn up with a dog! It has had a thorough refurbishment and is dog-friendly at the bar and outside, though not in the restaurant. There is a large garden at the rear.
☎ 01323 811244

A few doors down the road in the little lay-by, provisions can also be bought at the Laughton Village Shop & Post Office, usually open until 4pm.

Terrain: Flat paths, bridleways and tracks. Muddy in winter.
Livestock: None apart from horses using the bridleway.
Stiles and roads: No stiles. A small amount of road walking but along pavements.
Nearest vet: Cliffe Vets, 70 Springett Avenue, Ringmer, BN8 5QX.
☎ 01273 814590.

The Walk

. . . .

1 With your back to the pub turn right and then immediately right at the crossroads, to follow the lane (Shortgate Lane) signposted to Shortgate and Halland. Take the first footpath a few metres later on the right-hand side. Follow it on through the trees. After a while the path opens out from the wood with hedges on both sides and then becomes a

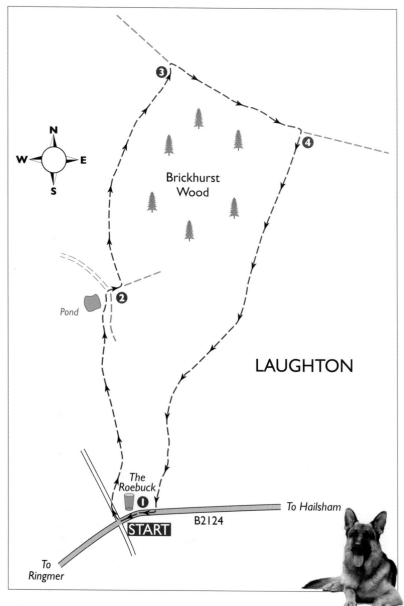

track. After a short while you pass a pond on the left-hand side with a convenient seat fashioned out of a tree trunk.

2 At the pond, where the track turns left, take the broad track on the right-hand side into the woods but then a few metres later take the signed footpath

on the immediate left into the woods. Continue along this path – in places the vegetation can encroach. Carry on to the far end where you come out onto a bridleway.

3 Turn right onto the bridleway. Ignore the few very small paths that lead into the wood on the right. Wait until you get to the main right-hand bridleway turn, this is marked by a large metal gate.

4 Turn right down this bridleway. Follow it to the far end. At the road turn right past the Post Office and a few metres later you'll be back at the Roebuck. *You will have seen the village sign, referring to the 'Village of the Buckle'. This is a reference to the buckle on the landowning Pelham family's coat of arms. This was a gift from King Edward III in reward for leading a group of local men to repulse a small French fleet that attempted to land on the nearby coast in 1356.*

16 LITLINGTON
2½ miles (4 km)

We discovered this village by accident when we stopped at the Plough & Harrow when other pubs or cafés in the more touristy places were full. We were so impressed we now often use it whenever we are in the area. Most people think of Litlington as a place for a riverside walk from nearby Alfriston, but although it's only a few houses scattered along the lane, it's well worth a visit in its own right. Its most famous resident was a Maria Fitzherbert. She got married in 1786 with the bride and groom using a false name; they left the church as Mr and Mrs Payne. Perhaps not that noteworthy except Mr Payne was actually the Prince Regent who later became George IV. One of their children was born in the village before the prince dumped Maria in favour of the Princess of Brunswick.

Start & Finish: The Plough & Harrow, The Street.
Sat Nav: BN26 5RE.
How to get there: On the A27 between Lewes and Eastbourne, at Drusilla's roundabout, take the southbound exit sign posted to Drusilla's Park and Alfriston. Then take the next left and after crossing the river, turn right then next right again. When you come to Litlington village, the pub is on the right-hand side at the far end of the village.
Parking: Either at the pub or in the village, though be cautious as the road is particularly narrow. If you are thinking of visiting Alfriston, this walk is ideal as parking in Alfriston is limited and costly.
OS Map: Explorer OL25 Eastbourne and Beachy Head.
Grid ref: TQ 523017.

THE PUB **THE PLOUGH & HARROW** is ideally placed for not only this walk but exploration of the surrounding area. Parts of the building date back to the 17th century. Dogs are welcome both inside and outside with water bowls and free treats on the bar. There is also a secluded dog friendly garden at the rear. ☎ 01323 870632 ⊕ ploughandharrowlitlington.co.uk

EAST SUSSEX – Dog Friendly Pub Walks

Terrain: Mostly flat paths.
Livestock: None.
Stiles and roads: No stiles. A little pavement walking in the village, and if taking the shortcut.
Nearest vet: Beechwood Veterinary Surgery, 37 Stafford Road, Seaford, BN25 1UE. ☎ 01323 893884.

The Walk

1 Walk to the far end of the pub car park. On the right-hand side there is a low step in the stone wall. Go through the step and turn left down the footpath. A few metres later you'll be at the end of the path.

2 At the end of the path turn left at the waymarker signed public footpath and then after another few metres turn right and cross the bridge over the river. At the other end of the bridge bear right and then turn right immediately so you have the riverbank on your right-hand side. You now just keep going in the same direction keeping the river on your right. After a mile you'll have the village of Alfriston on your left-hand side. Once you've passed the church on your left-hand side you come to a bridge over the river with white railings.

3 If you want to have a look at the village turn left here and take the path bearing left. It's an interesting place with a famous village green known as The Tye and some ancient houses. It's well worth a diversion to have a quick look. The dog friendly Shot Coffee House

offers a takeaway service or perhaps, if you have longer, visit the Tavern on the Tye which has a great terrace overlooking the green. To return to the walk keep going along the riverbank keeping the river on your right-hand side until you come to the next bridge.

4 Go through the gate, turn right, cross the river and turn right again through the gate with the river still on your right-hand side. All you are doing is just returning back down the other side of the river but it's great scenery and a really tranquil, peaceful place for a walk. See below if you wish to take the shortcut back to the start.** To continue along the riverside keep ahead. When you get back to Point 2, retrace your steps back up the path. However, don't go back to the pub car park, keep ahead until you come to the lane and here turn left. There is a short walk through the picturesque village on the pavement. At the end you'll find the church on the left, which is usually open from mid-morning until dusk.

5 If you appreciated a beer from the Long Man Brewery at the Plough & Harrow you now realise how close 'locally produced' can mean in Sussex. Keep to the grass verge and only a few metres further on the brewery is on the right-hand side. Although it's a working site, the brewery shop welcomes dogs and it's worth a quick look. Retracing your steps back into the village and your car, if you need some more refreshments the tea gardens on the left-hand side (closed Mondays except Bank Holidays) also welcome dogs.

**There is a shortcut but it is not suitable for larger dogs that you cannot assist over stiles. After point 4, when you get to a white bridge turn left down the path away from the river. Continue a short distance and as soon as you cross the stream turn right before you reach the lane. A few metres later cross the stile and follow the path keeping the hedge line on the left-hand side. At the end of the next field where it comes out at the lane, take the footpath on the immediate right. Cross the next stile and next field. At the end of that field cross another stile, turn left and follow the footpath alongside the left-hand field boundary. Keep following the footpath and where it comes out at the lane take the path parallel to the lane on its right-hand side. Where the path comes to an end there is a short distance of road walking as far as the church and point 5 on the main walk.

17 MICHELHAM PRIORY

3 miles (4.8 km)

This is a gentle walk through easy countryside from the village of Upper Dicker with the opportunity to take a look at the outside of ancient Michelham Priory. Much of the walk is along the Wealdway long-distance footpath. There are several stiles, two of which make this walk only suitable for dogs that you can carry over, although on our last visit there were informal ways around for larger dogs (through gaps or adjacent gates) but these cannot be guaranteed as permanent arrangements.

Start & Finish: The Plough, Coldharbour Road, Upper Dicker.
Sat Nav: BN27 3QJ.
How to get there: The village of Upper Dicker is signposted off the A22 near the Horsebridge roundabout close to Hailsham. The pub is on the right-hand side on Coldharbour Road, the main street through the village. It is at the far end if you are coming from the A222 direction.
Parking: There is plenty of on-street parking in the village or alternatively at the pub.
OS Map: Explorer OL25 Eastbourne & Beachy Head.
Grid ref: TQ 549096.

THE PUB | **THE PLOUGH** dates from the 1600s and features the usual wooden beams you'd expect, whilst outside there is a well tended garden and terrace seating. Award-winning chefs prepare everything fresh and produce is locally sourced where possible. Although much of the pub is given over to dining, dogs are welcome in the smaller bar area which contains comfy sofas next to the inglenook fireplace.
☎ 01323 844859 ⊕ plough-upperdicker.co.uk

Terrain: Easy gradients, mostly along footpaths. Some of the walk is low-lying and can be muddy after rain.
Livestock: None encountered but be mindful of any notices posted about waterfowl.
Stiles and roads: As mentioned in the introduction there are several stiles. If you do have difficulty with a larger dog and you have got as far as point 4 on the map (more than halfway round), take a look at the OS map and you will see there are alternative roads or tracks back to the main road through to the village which will save the walk becoming longer than you bargained for! There are a few very short sections of road walking.
Nearest vet: Chase Veterinary Centre, 89-91 Seaside, Eastbourne, BN22 7NL. ☎ 01323 639331.

The Walk

. . . .

❶ With your back to the pub turn left and walk along the pavement down the main road. Cross over at the zebra crossing and on the other side of the road carry on in the same direction. Just before you get to the village shop take the footpath marked Wealdway on the right-hand side. Cross the service road and follow the path next to the cottage opposite. Once you're out of the field continue ahead. Cross the first playing field. Where the playing fields divide, bear right and head diagonally across the right-hand playing field towards the left-hand side of the white pavilion at the far end. At the corner go to the gate and turn left onto the lane.

❷ Turn left down the drive to Michelham Priory if you wish to take a quick look. *The priory is the site of an Augustinian monastic house dating from 1229 and it still retains the country's largest medieval water-filled moat. The four-storey gatehouse dates from the 15th century and the*

bridge over the moat was built about 100 years later. You can take a look around the outside of the oak-framed 16th-century watermill. Fed from the moat it is in full working order with a waterwheel at the back of the mill. The property does not allow dogs further than the gatehouse. To continue the walk turn left out of the drive, continue along the lane, cross the bridge and take the footpath immediately on the right-hand side over the stile. Cross the short field and go through the next gate. Keep to the left-hand side of the field with the wood on your left-hand side. When you get to the next field boundary bear diagonally right across the

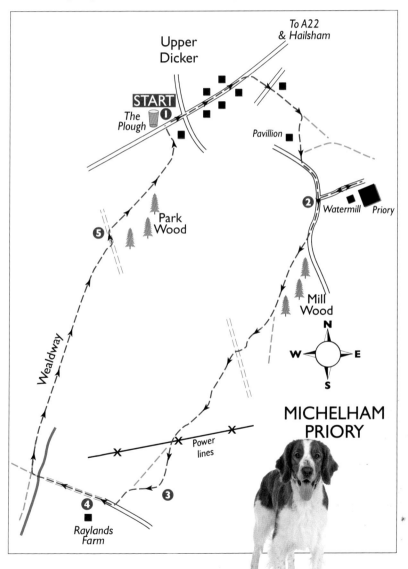

following field underneath the electricity wires; you are heading for the far right-hand corner of this field. At the far end cross the little bridge over the stream. Turn right. Immediately cross over the farm track. Follow the footpath waymarker along the right-hand side of the next field. You now keep following the footpath signs keeping ahead in the same direction. Cross the bridge at the end of the

field and follow the path through the little wood. At the end of the wood, go through the gate. Keep to the left-hand side of the next field and go through the next few gates still keeping the same direction. In the following field there are some benches on the left to sit and take in the views of the distant South Downs. Pass underneath the electricity lines. At this point the footpath has been diverted away from the right-of-way which crosses the field. The maintained path keeps to the left-hand side of the field boundary. A gate has been provided at the end. Go through the gate.

3 Once you have gone through the gate do not go straight ahead. Take the well-worn path as it bears right through the trees. Where it emerges follow the public footpath sign over the stile and then across the next field. The stile here has an interesting dog gate – push down on the left-hand side of the top bar of the stile and a like a see-saw the right-hand side rises to allow an animal through! Turn right along the lane.

4 Pass Raylands Farm on your left and keep going in the same direction. The track will soon meander into a path. As soon as you cross the river over a bridge there is a crossroads of paths immediately afterwards. Turn right following the Wealdway waymarker. You will now be following the Wealdway long-distance footpath across the fields all the way back towards the village.

5 When you come out onto a farm track next to a house on the left-hand side turn left and then immediately bear right again following the Wealdway sign. Keep to the right-hand side of the field next to the wood and either go through the gate or across the stile at the top, then carry on in the same direction down through the playing fields. At the next gate, bear left following the Wealdway waymarker down the footpath to bring you out to the main road. When you get to the main road turn right and the pub is almost immediately on your left.

18 RYE HARBOUR
2½ miles (4 km)

There is plenty to see on this walk through a landscape which has only existed for the last 600 years or so. Before that, where you are walking was a couple of miles out to sea. Shingle has been progressively deposited by the sea which caused the medieval port of Rye to block up (now two miles inland) which in turn saw the establishment of the community of Rye Harbour about 200 years ago. Today there is still fishing and commercial shipping, a lifeboat station, a Martello tower and an extensive nature reserve. There is a very large free car park which makes this walk a good option on busier days where parking is more limited elsewhere. Crowds may flock to famous Camber Sands only a few metres across the river but there's actually more to see at Rye Harbour.

Start & Finish: Rye Harbour Car Park, Harbour Road.
Sat Nav: TN31 7TU.
How to get there: From the A259 Hastings to Folkestone coastal road take the Rye Harbour turn on the outskirts of Rye. Follow the road to the far end through the village and the car park is signed on the right-hand side.
Parking: Park at the large, free public car park provided by the parish council situated in the middle of the village.
OS Map: Explorer 125 Romney Marsh, Rye & Winchelsea.
Grid ref: TQ942190.

THE PUB

THE WILLIAM THE CONQUEROR is a popular local institution and takes its name from a claim that this was the spot where the Normans invaded in 1066, although received wisdom has the landing place many miles along the coast at Pevensey. There is outdoor seating across the road close to the river, an ideal place to sit and watch the world go by.
☎ 01797 223315   ⊕ williamtheconqueror.co.uk.

Almost opposite, just over the flood bank and next to the new lifeboat station is the resolutely dog friendly **BOSUN'S BITE** café. Usually open daily except Christmas Day from 9am – 3pm. Expect homemade cooking with hounds welcome inside and out. ☎ 07834 730528. No website.

Terrain: Flat footpaths and private roads. Shingle banks if you want to explore the beach option.
Livestock: None.
Stiles and roads: No stiles. The only traffic allowed on the private roads are maintenance and works vehicles for the harbour and nature reserve so although you need to keep a look out, it's virtually traffic free.
Nearest vet: Cinque Ports Vets, Rye Veterinary Surgery, Cinque Ports Square, Rye, TN31 7AN. ☎ 01797 222265.

The Walk

1 Turn right out of the car park and take the second turning on the right (to the left of the holiday park entrance) down the private road with the Rye Harbour Nature Reserve entrance sign. Although the first right-hand turn into the holiday park is a public right-of-way (and gets you on the right path) it's easier to use the permissive path further along the private road. However, you can go a few metres into the park to take a circuit of the Martello tower. *Following the French Revolution, Napoleon Bonaparte declared war on Britain in 1793. To counter the threat, a line of forts and towers were built along the coast. The towers were based on a round tower at Cape Mortella in Corsica which held out against British attack in 1794. 'Mortella' became 'Martello' and 74 of them were built between Folkestone and Seaford between 1805 and 1810. This is tower number 28 dating from 1806 and was built to guard the harbour. Although derelict it retains many features lost in other towers through neglect or conversion. There was once a bridge over the moat with access to the tower at the first floor level.* Returning to the private road walk as far as the first path on the right.

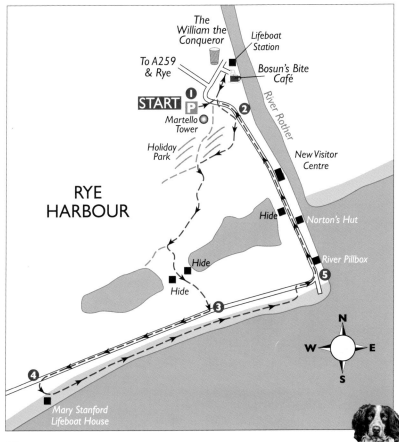

The William the
Conqueror

Lifeboat
Station

To A259
& Rye

Bosun's Bite
Café

START P ❶

❷

River Rother

Martello
Tower

Holiday
Park

New Visitor
Centre

RYE
HARBOUR

Hide

Norton's Hut

Hide

River Pillbox

Hide

❺

Hide

❸

N
W E
S

❹

Mary Stanford
Lifeboat House

❷ Take the footpath which runs on an embankment keeping the holiday park on the right-hand side. A short distance later follow the path as it turns left out across the marshes and through the nature reserve. *The reserve consists of over a thousand acres of shingle, saltmarsh, salty lagoons, freshwater gravel pits and reed beds and is best known for its breeding birdlife.* At the next junction of paths again bear left, passing bird hides on either side shortly after.

❸ When you get to another private tarmac road turn right (or go a few metres further up the boardwalk onto the beach and head right along the beach) as far as the Mary Stanford lifeboat house. *This empty Grade II-listed building stands as a reminder of the worst ever disaster in the history of the RNLI. In 1928 the whole of the 17-man crew – virtually the entire male fishing population of the village – were needlessly drowned when the lifeboat, named* Mary Stanford, *capsized after it had been launched into a fierce gale to save the crew of a stricken ship in the channel. Unbeknown to the brave lifeboatmen the crew had*

already been rescued and in the midst of the storm they were unaware of the attempts to recall them.

4 You now retrace your steps, again either along the private road or beach, back past point 3 and on towards the river mouth. You won't make it all the way there on the beach, just before the end you will have to come back inland and join the tarmac road.

5 When you get to the end of the road with the River Rother opposite you, you turn left and make your way back to Rye Harbour village. *The Second World War pillbox on the right is exceptionally well preserved and was built, about 150 years later, for exactly the same reason as the earlier Martello Tower. It still retains the concrete tables with triangular indentations designed to mount Vickers machine guns in the event of German invasion. The walls and roof are made of shell-proof 1m concrete.* Continuing along the walk there is Norton's Hut on the right and another bird hide on the left. If the tide is high you may see ships from the Rye fishing fleet passing, taking advantage of the tidal water channel. When you are back at point 2 keep to the raised right-hand path and follow that round, this will bring you out at the pub and the café avoiding the road.

19 SEAFORD HEAD & CUCKMERE WEST

3½ miles (5.6 km)

This is a walk with a view so famous it's claimed over 400,000 visitors come here each year from across the world to see it for themselves. It's the iconic view from Seaford Head looking down over Cuckmere Haven with the picturesque Coastguard Cottages in the foreground and the towering white cliffs of the Seven Sisters marching into the seascape. Don't be put off by the number of people who come to visit, our route uses a little known 'back door' car park. The best time to come is late in the day. Of course make sure you have enough daylight to complete the walk, but the coachloads of tourists will have gone and on your return you'll see the view in the best possible light as the low sun illuminates the scene as it sets in the west.

Start & Finish: South Hill Barn Car Park, Chyngton Lane.
Sat Nav: BN25 4JA.
How to get there: Chyngton Lane is blocked to vehicular traffic off the main A259 Seaford to Eastbourne Road. The easiest way is to turn off

the A259 when it has become Sutton Avenue in Seaford town centre and then take the second left onto Southdown Road. You then take the sixth turn on the left into Chyngton Road which you follow through into Chyngton Way. At the far end you turn up Chyngton Lane which is a concrete track and leads to the top of the hill where there is car parking on the left and right-hand side.

Parking: South Hill Barn Car Park is surprisingly quiet bearing in mind it is both free of charge and excellently positioned so close to such a famous view. If for any reason the car park is full, unfortunately you will have to go back down to Chyngton Way and walk up the hill.

OS Map: Explorer OL25 Eastbourne & Beachy Head.

Grid ref: TV504981.

Terrain: Broad and wide paths and tracks.
Livestock: None.
Stiles and roads: No stiles or road walking.
Nearest vet: Beechwood Veterinary Surgery, 37 Stafford Road, Seaford, BN25 1UE. ☎ 01323 893884.

THE PUB **THE CUCKMERE INN** sits in a great location overlooking the South Downs National Park with views from its outside seats looking across the meandering River Cuckmere. Dogs are allowed in the bar area. Food is only served outside to the tables closest to the pub – which can get very busy on summer weekends.
☎ 01323 892247 ⊕ vintageinn.co.uk

The Walk

1️⃣ Go through the exit at the far end of the car park. Take the track in the middle of the two concrete roads (these are a redundant turning circle). Keep ahead along the track, and soon one of England's most iconic views will open up before you. *The Coastguard Cottages were built in the 1830s to both combat smuggling and help save lives at sea. The adjacent cable hut is one of the few remaining cable stations on the South Coast where, in the early 20th century, telegraph messages from London were converted to undersea cable messages and retransmitted to France. The scene has featured on TV, films and commercials countless times. The scene is often used as a film double for the White Cliffs of Dover. Erosion here keeps the chalk a photogenic sparkling white whereas coastal defences at Dover around the real White Cliffs stop erosion and encourage vegetation to grow which takes the shine off the white. Behind them, each of the Seven Sisters has their own*

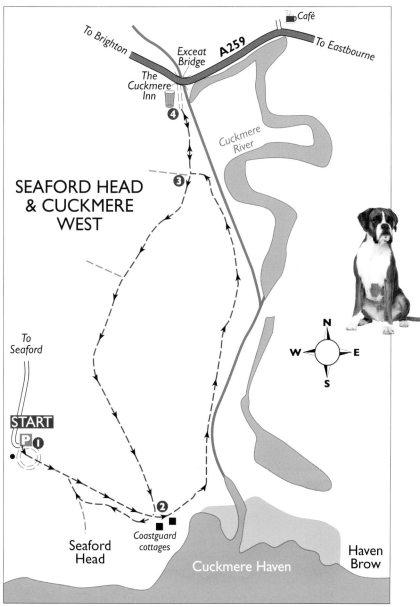

name. Haven Brow, the highest of them at 253 feet is first, followed in order by Short Brow, Rough Brow, Brass Point, Flagstaff Point, Baily's Brow and Went Hill Brow. Head to the very bottom with the iconic Coastguard Cottages on your right-hand side.

❷ Head down to the beach. *At very low tide you might see the remains of PLUTO, an acronym for Pipe Line Under The Ocean. This was laid along the bottom of the English Channel to pump fuel to France to support the allied army following the invasion of Europe after D-Day in 1944.* When you get to the river follow it inland. You will soon find a raised footpath. Follow the footpath inland.

❸ When you come to a crossroads of paths turn right and you will soon emerge into the car park of the Cuckmere Inn.

❹ Retracing your steps, keep ahead at point 3 along the Vanguard Way long-distance footpath. This will finally bring you out back at the Coastguard Cottages at point 2. Now turn right, back up the hill. On the return you can take a path through the grass which runs roughly parallel with the track on the left-hand side – perhaps it's a bit easier for tired paws at the end of the day.

20 THREE LEG CROSS & BEWL WATER
3, 4 or 6 miles (4.8, 6.4 or 9.7 km)

However you do this walk (and we've got three versions of it) the big attraction is enjoying the peace and tranquillity of the largest stretch of inland open water in the South East. Bewl Water is an artificial reservoir created in the 1970s when the River Bewl was dammed and the valleys behind it flooded. The reservoir now supports a sizable leisure industry of sailing, water sports, walking and hiking. Our walk sticks to the quieter part of Bewl Water, and to include a little variety you can even include a boat trip.

Start & Finish: The Bull Inn, Huntley Mill Road, Three Leg Cross.
Sat Nav: TN5 7HH.
How to get there: From the southbound A21 from Tonbridge, Rosemary Lane is a small right-hand turn about a mile before the Flimwell crossroads. If travelling north from Hastings it's a left-hand turn a mile after Flimwell. Follow the lane (you'll pass the reservoir on your right), keep going to the end of the road then turn right and then next right. When you get to Three Leg Cross turn left and the pub is a few metres further on, on the right-hand side.
Parking: At the pub or unrestricted on-road parking nearby.
OS Map: Explorer 136 High Weald. **Grid ref:** TQ 685311.

THE PUB

THE BULL INN was built between 1385 and 1425 and is reputed to be one of the oldest dwelling places in the county, although it only became a pub towards the end of the 19th century. You'll find stone-flagged floors, real fires and timber beams all set in four acres where there is outside

seating to the front and back complete with dovecote and (fenced off) duck pond. It feels remarkably un-commercialised and is well worth a visit.
☎ 01580 200586 ⊕ facebook.com/TheBullInnThreeLegCrossTicehurst

In contrast **THE BELL** at Ticehurst is only two minutes' drive down the lane (turn left at the end). With parts dating from 1296 and licensed since 1495, it was named, as was the tradition at the time, after the single bell in the village church. It has recently found a name for itself as a boutique hotel. However, unlike so many other similar places it hasn't turned its back on its roots. With the promise that dogs are always welcome they are allowed in the main bar which commendably hasn't been pushed out by a restaurant and relegated to just a few stools. There's also a good sized courtyard at the back and you'll find dog water bowls inside and out. Local beers are from the Cellar Head Brewing Company.
☎ 01580 200300 ⊕ thebellinticehurst.com

Terrain: Mostly wide tracks around the lake, one slightly steep climb up a footpath and a stretch along a quiet country lane. Dogs must be kept clear of anglers and wildlife and kept out of the water at all times. Don't let them drink the water where an algae bloom is present as it can cause fatal toxins when ingested. Take stout waterproof footwear, no matter what time of year the bottom of the path at point 6 always seems to be resolutely wet and muddy.
Livestock: No livestock, but you may encounter horse riders and waterfowl.
Stiles and roads: No stiles. Some walking along a quiet country lane.
Nearest vet: Cinque Ports Vets, Cranbrook Road, Hawkhurst, Kent, TN18 5EE. ☎ 01580 752187.

The Walk

❶ Turn sharp left out of the pub and walk down the lane through the village. Pass Tinkers Lane on the right. Turn left at the first footpath sign in front of a set of white weatherboarded cottages. This will take you down a private lane towards Hazelhurst Farm. However, as the signage confirms, it is a right-of-way as a footpath.

❷ When you get to a cattle grid and the concrete track bears left, bear sharp left onto the footpath signposted 'Bridleway and round Bewl Water walk'. Follow this bridleway until you have dropped down a couple of steps and you are facing a bridge across the stream.

❸ Take the footpath that turns right just before the bridge. You will soon have a great waterside walk with the lake on your left-hand side. After a short while you

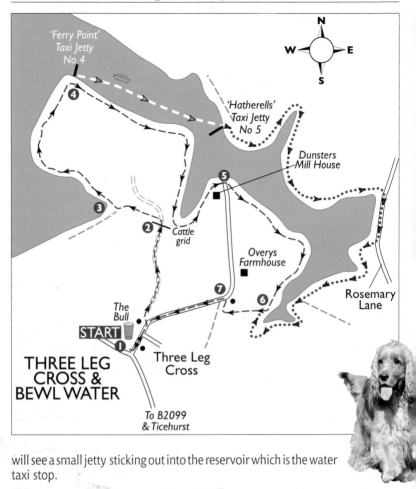

will see a small jetty sticking out into the reservoir which is the water taxi stop.

4 This is water taxi stop numb.... ...ry Point on the taxi schedule, see p95 if you want to take the boat option.** If you're not taking the water taxi, continue around the path keeping the water on your left. Follow the path as it runs down the side of an inlet. Ignore the Bewl Water bridle path sign you come to after a gate on the right-hand side and continue along the ahead. Carry on ahead and round the other side of the inlet, again with water on your left-hand side. You'll soon be walking through woods but still with the water on your left. Take a note of the large tiles hung house on your right-hand side. *This is the 14th-century Dunsters Mill House. It used to stand on your left-hand side where there is now nothing but water. When the valley was flooded in 1973 the house was moved piece by piece, over two years, to safety half a mile up the hill, although its farm, millpond and waterwheel were lost for ever, submerged by the lake.*

⑤ When you come to the sunken lane, drop down, turn right and then immediately sharp left to keep along the reservoir path.

⑥ When you get almost to the end of the next inlet take the first footpath on the right-hand side. It will start to climb up the hill. Warning - it can be very muddy here even in summer after rain. Follow the path as it turns right at the top and then for a few metres becomes a tarmac drive. At the very top, when you emerge out onto the lane, turn left.

❼ Walk back up the lane until you get back to Three Leg Cross, the pub and the start.

** A dog friendly water taxi service is available on Bewl Water 7 days a week between 9am and 4pm. Telephone in advance of your walk to confirm the service is running and book your pick up time from Jetty No 4 Ferry Point. ☎ 01892 890000 Ask to be taken to Catherells which is Jetty No 5. When you have got off the boat, walk up the path a few metres and then turn right onto the round reservoir path. Continue with the water on your right-hand side until you come out into Rosemary Lane. Turn right at the lane. Walk along the lane and where it starts to rise away from the reservoir, go through the gate on the right-hand side. Keep going along the round reservoir path. You will later be taking the second footpath on the left-hand side. This is point 6 on the map. The turning is shortly after when the path you are on turns sharply right as it crosses a stream.

To make an even longer walk of about 6 miles, take the water taxi option as above but when you get to point 6 on the map stay on the round reservoir path. Keeping the water on your right-hand side go past point 5 back to point 4 and then retrace your steps back to point 1.

A SELECTION OF OTHER DOG FRIENDLY PUBS IN EAST SUSSEX

ALFRISTON – Star Inn
BARCOMBE – Anchor Inn
BARCOMBE CROSS – Royal Oak
BRIGHTON – Evening Star
BRIGHTON – Basketmakers Arms
BURWASH – Rose & Crown
CROWBOROUGH –Wheatsheaf
EAST DEAN – Tiger Inn
EASTBOURNE – Crown
EAST HOATHLY – Kings Head
ERIDGE – Huntsman
FOREST ROW – Chequers Inn
HADLOW DOWN – New Inn
HAILSHAM – The George
HASTINGS – Jenny Lind
HASTINGS – Jolly Fisherman

HERSTMONCEUX – Brewers Arms
HIGH ROCKS – High Rocks Inn
HOVE – Foghorn
ICKLESHAM – Queens Head
JEVINGTON – Eight Bells
LEWES – Gardener's Arms
NEWICK – Crown
PEASMARSH – Horse & Cart
PEVENSEY – Royal Oak & Castle
RYE – Ypres Castle Inn
ST LEONARDS – Tower
SEAFORD – Steamworks
UCKFIELD – Alma Arms
WINCHELSEA – New Inn